MOUNT MARATHON

Third Edition

Mount Marathon
Alaska's Great Footrace

Millie Spezialy

ALASKA
NORTHWEST
BOOKS

Text © 2013 by Millie Spezialy

Photographs © 2013 by the photographers as noted below:

Ron Niebrugge, front cover; Carol Sheridan, pages ii-iii, vi, 66, 74, 77, 85, 10; Seward Community Library/ Alaska's Digital Archives, page 2; Anchorage Museum of History & Art Library Archives, Alaska's Digital Archives, page 6; Jackie Pels/ Hardscratch Press, pages 8, 13, 15, 21b, 21c, 21d, 25; Alaska State Library, page 11; University of Alaska Anchorage, page 21a; Lewis Haines Family, pages 18, 84; University of Alaska Fairbanks, pages 23a, 23b; Seward Phoenix Log, pages 26, 52; William Spencer Family, page 28; Bill Spencer, page 31; Anchorage Daily News, pages 35, 88; TSS Photography, pages 39, 42, 49, 54, 59, 63, 80, 87b, 90a, 90b, 95, 104; 94, 104, 108, 85b, 88a, 88b, 92c; Laura Gardner, 45; John Hilsinger, page 61; Patricia Anderson, page 87a; Kopsack Family, page 92b; Deb Essex, page 93c; Mary Hensel, page 108; Chris Griswold, page 112; Loren Holmes, page 113; Allyson Youngblood of Alaska Mountain Rescue Group, page 122.

All rights reserved. No part of this book may be reproduced, stored in a retrieval system, or transmitted in any form or by any means, electronic, mechanical, photocopying, recording, or otherwise, without written permission from the publisher.

Library of Congress Control Number: 2013936870

Alaska Northwest Books®
An imprint of Graphic Arts Books
P.O. Box 56118
Portland, OR 97238-6118
(503) 254-5591
www.graphicartsbooks.com

Interior Design: Brad Greene
Cover Design: Vicki Knapton

Cover photo: Runners ascend the summit during the 2002 women's race.
Pages ii and iii: Runners on a ridge nearing the summit of Mount Marathon. They go up the gravel and come down on the snow.

Contents

1 The History of Seward and the Mount Marathon Race 1

2 The Early Years of the Race: 1915–43 7

3 The Race—and the Prize—Grow: 1946–61 13

4 Race Participation Expands 19
    The First Women in the Race 20
    The 1964 Earthquake 22

5 Record Runners 27
    Top Record Setters 27
    Ten Top Finishes... 29
    Age Group Record Holders 2007–12 69

6 For Love of the Race 83
    Mountain Running Families.. 83
    Inspirational Runners.. 94
    Colorful Men of the Mountain 104
    Senior Runners... 105
    Faces Behind the Race 109

7 2012—A Year to Remember 119

8 Race Rules and Annual Winners 129
    How to Apply 129
    Top 100 Times on Mount Marathon 132

View from the summit of Mount Marathon with Seward and Resurrection Bay below.

The History of Seward and the Mount Marathon Race

The Legend of Mount Marathon

Beer, bets, and bravado flowed freely at a local bar as Seward residents prepared to celebrate the Fourth of July in 1909. According to local legend, the residents wanted something more challenging than the greased pole climb and tug-of-war contest. "How about a grueling footrace?" asked the man with a bushy beard. Heads nodded in agreement. A short, bald man jumped up and pointed out the window to the mountain towering behind the town. Then he slapped a bill on the bar. "I've got a hundred dollars says nobody can run up and down that hill in under an hour." Some say Al Taylor, a dog musher known for his speed and stamina, took the challenge. He was so sure of success that he countered the offer: "If I can't get up and down that hill in under an hour, the drinks are on me." The first race took place long before spandex or running shoes. Taylor, dressed in his Sunday-best white shirt, woolen trousers, and leather boots, ran up the dusty street and into the woods. Within an hour he reappeared. Shouts erupted from the bar patrons, who flooded outside to cheer Taylor on. Watches were checked and the verdict given. He missed the goal. By minutes. A dusty, tired, and thirsty Taylor sauntered into the bar and bought drinks for the house.

1903: The Founding of Seward

Seward's founding fathers came to the shores of Resurrection Bay seeking jobs, challenge, and freedom in the Territory of Alaska. They arrived by boat on August 28, 1903, to build a railroad terminus on the land at the head of Resurrection Bay. Ten days after their arrival, the pioneers had built winter quarters for all the inhabitants, and a schoolhouse was under

2 Mount Marathon

Patriotism ran strong and deep in the hardy men and women who founded Seward. Local children get ready to carry the flag in Seward's Fourth of July Parade before the start of the race. Today, the parade is held between the women's and men's races.

construction to accommodate the twelve children of the community. That summer, the settlers, thankful for the freedom and opportunities they found in Alaska, celebrated their first Independence Day by gathering in white tents on the beach for speeches, food, drinks, and rifle shots in place of fireworks. Patriotism ran strong and deep in these hardy men and women. They named their city after William H. Seward, Abraham Lincoln's secretary of state, who had initiated the purchase of Alaska from Russia in 1867. Then to honor the first five presidents, they named the east-west–running streets Washington, Adams, Jefferson, Madison, and Monroe.

Mountain runners and Seward pioneers share many of the same traits. Both find renewal in the midst of nature, hard work, and giving back to the community. Athletes promote a healthy lifestyle while interacting with nature, and many work to maintain and preserve wilderness trails. The spirit of giving back displayed by settlers in the many fraternal organizations founded in 1904 to help people in need lives on today in the many Seward volunteers who work year-round to prepare for the Mount Marathon Race.

Mount Marathon is the oldest mountain race held in Alaska and the third oldest footrace in the United States (only the Boston Marathon and California's Dipsea Race are older). This unique race has grown steadily in popularity since the first official race was run in 1915. Through economic downturns, natural disasters, and population loss, the folks in Seward—a town of 2,500—have never lost their enthusiasm for sponsoring this unique event. It's the main attraction for their Independence Day celebration, which also features music, food, fireworks, and a parade down city streets. The race has grown from three competitors in 1915 to more than nine hundred today.

Runners migrate to Seward in spring to practice on the mountain, where they mingle with Seward rescue workers, sharpening their rescue skills, as both prepare for the big race.

The Seward Volunteer Fire Department helps a few injured runners off the mountain each season, as well as a few hikers who don't realize how dangerous the trail can be, get paralyzed by fright, and call for help.

About the Race Course

The Fourth of July race takes place on a mountain that dominates the Seward landscape and is visible from any point in town. The first unofficial race up the mountain in 1909 was billed as a marathon run. One year later, Seward folks were calling the mountain Marathon Hill, which quickly evolved into its current name, Mount Marathon.

The starting line for the race is 30 feet above sea level and racers climb another 2,992 feet to the summit. The total distance is just a little over three miles, but it's a daunting climb. The average trail angle is thirty-eight degrees but many sections are a scramble up sixty-degree slopes.

Competitors had only three rules to worry about in the early years of the race: start at the flagpole in front of the Bank of Seward on Adams and Fourth Street, circle the rock on the peak, and return to the starting point. What they did in between the three checkpoints was up to each runner. It was not unusual to see runners cutting through backyards, jumping over fences, and upsetting clotheslines on their quest for glory.

The Mount Marathon Race starts with a half-mile road run before the steep climb up the rocky bluffs; then the scramble up the dirt through trees and rocky ridges to the checkpoint at the top; a free fall down ice, snow, and shale; the descent over the waterfall and cliffs at the bottom; and finally, the mad dash down the street to the finish line.

Some seasoned runners might not consider that a difficult challenge. But competitive runners are quick to point out that there's a thin line between winning and staying alive on this course. Conditions on the mountain change quickly. After a few days of rain, runners crawl and claw their way up the muddy slope and slick shale. In 1994 the women's route through the trees resembled a long, vertical mud slide. The pitch in this area is so steep runners place their hands on the ground to gain leverage and balance.

Snow conditions at the steep, crevasse-filled snowfield near the summit are always daunting, and ice beneath the snow makes it almost impossible to keep your footing. To achieve record runs, competitors must glissade down the snowfield at breakneck speeds before bounding out onto the shale in twenty-foot strides, a virtual free fall. Go slow and competitors fly by; go fast and you might tumble head over heels into the scree. Many runners leave flesh and blood scattered over the downhill route, as the mountain has been known to bite chunks out of rear ends, slash hands and shins, and tear away knee cartilage. In 1994, Danielle Winn slid feet first down the snow out of control, went over a rock face, and fell thirty feet. She survived the thirty-foot fall and was presented the Purple Heart Award.

Hot weather can humble a runner. In 1984, temperatures hovered around 85°F by the time the men's race started. Sam Young's winning run in 50:47 left him dehydrated, suffering from heat exhaustion and blistered feet. When he passed out one foot over the finish line, his friends pulled him over to the curb and wet him down with a water hose. When someone noticed, a couple hours later, that Young was still unresponsive they became alarmed and rushed him to the hospital, where he was hooked up to an IV drip and rehydrated.

Competitors are drawn to this unique race for many reasons: to set a record, flirt with danger, as a personal challenge, or just as a fun way to celebrate the Fourth of July. John Smith, alias Elvis, who skipped across the finish line wearing a blue rhinestone suit, was not shy about expressing his feelings about the Mount Marathon Race. On a runner's high after completing the run, he told an *Anchorage Daily News* reporter, "I love this race. There's nothing like it. I'd like to do it until the pall bearers take me down."

Seward girls dressed in their Sunday best for their race on the Fourth of July.

The Early Years of the Race: 1915–43

R Indicates a new course record.
A runner's finish time is given in hours-minutes-seconds: 00:00:00

1915	James Walters	01:02:00	**1928**	Ephraim Kalmakoff	00:52:35 R
1916	Alec Bolan	00:55:12R	**1929**	Ephraim Kalmakoff	00:55:13
1917	Tom Hardoff	00:57:39	**1930**	Ephraim Kalmakoff	00:54:00
1918	Joe Karaoff	00:58:30	**1931**	William Kanyak	00:56:24
1919	D. Mautino	01:06:45	**1932–38**	no races held	
1920	seven-mile flatland run		**1939**	Johnny Hughes	00:58:55
1921-24	no race held		**1940**	Johnny Hughes	01:05:00
1925	Ed Vogel	00:57:40	**1941**	Oscar Wilson	01:09:23
1926	Eric Eckman	00:58:26	**1942**	no race held	
1927	Eric Eckman	01:01:17	**1943**	Roger Peck	01:10:15

> "Give me men to match my mountains."
> Mount Marathon Race slogan

The first official race in 1915 was won by James Walters, who missed the elusive hour barrier by a mere two minutes. One year later all three competitors finished in less than sixty minutes. Alec Bolan won in a time of 55:12; James Walters placed second in 55:56, and Al Taylor was third in 55:59. Bolan pulled off the win by outsmarting the field. He bridged a creek at the base of the mountain with a board and grabbed the lead. A deafening cheer erupted from the crowds lining the street as all three competitors sprinted toward the finish line. Money exchanged hands along the boardwalk as side bets were collected and paid off.

Word spread quickly through Seward in 1917 that two Russian employees of the railroad construction gang were practicing on the mountain, getting ready for the Fourth of July race. Madsen and Taylor, local men, showed up to challenge the newcomers. The extra training paid off for the Russians who walked away with one hundred dollars

---

★ Jesse Lee Home ★

In 1925 about one hundred children arrived in Seward to take up residence at the newly completed Jesse Lee Home in Seward. Two orphanages—the Jesse Lee at Unalaska and the Lavinia Wallace Young in Nome—were consolidated and relocated to Seward to be closer to transportation and supply lines. The citizens of Seward supported the move by donating and clearing one hundred acres of land needed for the project. In 1928, Ephraim Kalmakoff would be the first—but not the last—Jesse Lee Home student to win the Mount Marathon Race. Athletes from the Home dominated the race for the next fifteen years.

Ephraim Kalmakoff and brothers Mike and Inikente had entered the Home in Unalaska in 1924 after the death of their parents from tuberculosis. Mike died in Seward in 1928 from the same disease, at the age of thirteen. Ephraim's younger brother, Inikente, would later win the 1944 race while serving as a private in the Army at the age of twenty-five.

Ephraim Kalmakoff, at age thirteen.

and fifty dollars for their first- and second-place wins. The mood on the street was somber; Seward folks had bet heavily on local favorites, Madsen and Taylor, who finished third and fourth.

The 1919 race was memorable because half the field of four competitors got lost on the mountain; one on the way up and one on the way down. But D. Mautino, a marathon runner and soldier stationed in Seward who had practiced on the mountain, ran away with first place in a time of 1:06:45 and took home seventy-five dollars and a new suit from Seward pioneer retailer Brown and Hawkins.

After a five-year hiatus due to World War I, five competitors showed up for the 1925 run. Most folks in town didn't think forty-year-old, graying-at-the-temples Ed Vogel stood a chance of winning the race, which was by all accounts a duel for control. Ed Vogel and Eric Eckman, a twenty-five-year-old Swedish immigrant, ran side by side up Jefferson Street and Lowell Canyon Road. Eckman managed to pull ahead on the climb up and reached the rock turn-around at the summit ahead of Vogel. Bounding over the shale like a wild man, taking enormous risks, Vogel caught up with Eckman at the bottom of the mountain. The two ran through the muddy Seward streets neck and neck when Vogel poured on one last burst of speed and won by ten seconds in a time of 57:40. He paused to light a cigarette before stepping into the nearest bar, where the older crowd lined up to buy him drinks. Even though most of the men lost money because they'd bet on young Eckman, they reveled in Vogel's victory.

One year later in 1926, the tables were turned when Eckman, who kicked a mountain goat off the uphill trail, grabbed first place in 58:36, a full twelve minutes ahead of Vogel. The young Swede walked away with three hundred dollars and a new suit. Not bad for an hour's work.

Eckman was favored to win again in 1927, even though there were rumblings of a new rival. *Gateway*, the local newspaper, announced that a younger, faster competitor was training hard for the Fourth of July race: "Ephraim Kalmakoff will take a whirl at the pot of gold."

The younger, faster racer was a thirteen-year-old boy from the Sugpiat (Alutiiq) village of Chignik on the Alaska Peninsula. He had heard about the Mount Marathon Race soon after his arrival from Unalaska in 1925 and was eager to participate. He trained diligently for the 1927 race, but when the race was rescheduled to be run on a Sunday, he faced a dilemma: he didn't feel right about running on the Sabbath. When he asked one of his teachers what he should do, the man told him to do what he thought was right.

Ephraim thought he could win, but didn't feel good about running on Sunday and bowed out of the race. Without Ephraim in the race, Eric Eckman became the first two-time consecutive winner.

In 1928 the course changed when the starting line was moved to Fourth and Washington, increasing the distance of the run by three blocks.

Eckman was the odds-on favorite to win his third Mount Marathon Race. Although Kalmakoff posted fast times on practice runs, doubters questioned whether the slender, five-foot-five boy was capable of beating grown men.

On the Fourth of July all eyes were on young, fourteen-year-old Kalmakoff as he ran up Fourth Avenue dressed in his Boy Scout uniform. He pulled ahead of Eckman on Lowell Canyon Road and disappeared into the trees at the base of the mountain. He was first to reach the summit, first to the base of the mountain, and first over the finish line in a record breaking time of 52:35. Inikente Kalmakoff, eyes sparkling with admiration, had good reason to be proud of his big brother: Kalmakoff had just set a new course record. He remains the youngest Mount Marathon winner and his record, which stood for twenty-nine years, is the longest held record in the history of the race.

A dejected Eckman confessed to a *Gateway* reporter, "I just knew he was too good for me, I gave up before I started."

Later that day Kalmakoff was honored at a celebration at the Jesse Lee Home, which lasted long past curfew and included sandwiches, ice cream, cookies, and hot chocolate. The one hundred dollar prize money and gifts that Kalmakoff won were a big incentive for him to train and run again in 1929 and 1930. He won both years and became the first three-time consecutive winner in race history.

When you look at Kalmakoff's ancestry, it's no surprise that he would win a race requiring endurance, stamina, agility, and speed. His ancestors—the Sugpiat (Alutiiq) and Chugach people—had climbed the mountains surrounding Resurrection Bay for thousands of years harvesting the resources. Living a subsistence lifestyle kept them fit long before fitness coaches, athletic shoes, and sports drinks appeared on the scene.

★ Benny Benson ★

Another Home student and friend of Kalmakoff's from Chignik, Benjamin (Benny) Benson, placed second in the 1928 race in a time of 55:17. Although Benson was a good athlete, he is most celebrated and remembered as the boy who designed the Alaska Flag, eight stars of gold (the Big Dipper) on a field of dark blue.

It wasn't until fourteen years after Alaska became a US Territory in 1912 that anyone noticed that the Territory had no flag. The American Legion Posts around the Territory jumped in to remedy the situation by sponsoring a contest for a flag design. When the telegram announcing Benson's win reached his Jesse Lee Home classroom on April 21, 1927, Benson stood mute in shock, as his classmates applauded. Benson's design was adopted as the Alaska State Flag when Alaska became the forty-ninth state in 1959.

Benny Benson and his Alaska flag.

In 1931 Kalmakoff ran his last Mount Marathon Race in 59:51, three minutes behind William Kanyak, a friend and fellow Home resident. Kalmakoff look tired. His cheeks were flushed and he was breathing hard. Many thought that he'd exhausted himself on the mountain, but his fatigue was probably due to tuberculosis. He never ran the mountain again, and died of tuberculosis on May 18, 1937, at the age of twenty-four. His legacy of wins on Mount Marathon is still recognized and celebrated in Seward and by the mountain running community in Alaska.

After Kalmakoff's death, folks in Seward blamed the arduous Mount Marathon Race for his illness, which may have influenced the decision to cancel the race from 1932 to 1938, but others lay the blame for the race hiatus to the deepening national and local depression.

The Race—and the Prize—Grow: 1946–61

In 1941 the Seward Volunteer Firemen Association set up a lottery to sell chances on guessing the winning time for the race down to the tenth of a second, with money raised used for cash prizes and race expenses. By 1950 the first-place winner received twenty-five hundred dollars, a sum equal to many Seward men's wages for a year. With so much money at stake, a few men entered the race without training for the arduous climb and had to be helped down the mountain. The race committee responded by hiring a doctor to give physicals at the starting line.

A few days before the 1963 Mount Marathon run, three young women from Seward signed up for the race. Although race officials protested, there were no rules prohibiting women from competition.

1944–61

1944 Inikente Kalmakoff	00:59:59		**1953** Ralph Hatch	00:54:56	
1945 Mainhardt Bredt	01:01:11		**1954** Sven Johansson	00:53:20	R
1946 Ralph Hatch	00:59:58		**1955** Sven Johansson	00:57:09	
1947 Ralph Hatch	00:58:13		**1956** Sven Johansson	00:52:59	
1948 Ralph Hatch	00:57:31		**1957** Sven Johansson	00:51:40	R
1949 Ralph Hatch	01:06:52		**1958** Sven Johansson	00:52:45	
1950 Ralph Hatch	00:58:10		**1959** Sven Johansson	00:50:48	
1951 Don Stickman	00:56:38		**1960** Dick Kopsack	00:55:16	
1952 Don Stickman	00:53:36	R	**1961** Norman Roberts	00:51:02	

Ralph Hatch

One reason for the upswing in the number of runners and spectators after 1946 was due to the excitement Ralph Hatch brought to the race. Between 1946 and 1950, Hatch became the first five-time consecutive Mount Marathon winner. Born in Unalaska, he moved to Seward in 1930 with his Aleut parents, who worked and lived at the Jesse Lee Home.

As Hatch's fame grew, runners from around the state headed to Seward on the Fourth of July to test themselves against the local hero. Hatch welcomed the competition and graciously took new runners up the mountain to familiarize them with the trail.

Don Stickman, a commercial pilot and trapper, was the first out-of-town runner to fly his own plane into Seward for the race. He arrived at midnight in 1950, one day before the race. Within minutes, he set off to climb Mount Marathon, got lost, and wandered around the slopes for hours. On the day of the race he followed Hatch on the uphill section, to learn the way. At the summit, Stickman bolted past Hatch. They passed the lead back and forth between tumbles in the sharp shale. Then Stickman made a fatal error: he paused for water halfway down the mountain. Hatch took to the air, flew past, and won the race.

In 1951–52 Stickman trained diligently, determined to give Hatch a run for the money. Stickman, an Athabascan Indian from Ruby, Alaska,

The Race—and the Prize—Grow: 1946–61   15

Hometown hero Ralph Hatch—first man to win six Mount Marathon Races.

knew he had to pull ahead on the uphill, "Because," he told a *Gateway* reporter, "there isn't a man alive who could beat him [Hatch] on the way down." His training strategies worked and Stickman won both years.

After trailing Stickman over the finish line for two years, Hatch didn't plan for it to happen again. In 1953 he upped his climbs up the mountain, sometimes carrying twenty-five pounds of rocks in a backpack. It paid off. He won the race and ran a personal best in 54:56, becoming the first man to win six Mount Marathon Races. A disappointed Stickman, who took a bad fall near the summit, came in third.

In an unusual stroke of luck, Hatch also held the winning lottery ticket: he'd picked 54:56 as the winner's finish time. Ever the gentleman, he refused the lottery money and gave it to the next closest guess.

Hatch wasn't always in a hurry to reach the summit of Mount Marathon. As a special treat for his two- and three-year-old daughters, he carried them up the mountain in a backpack, one at a time, for a father-daughter picnic.

Hatch, a shy, reserved World War II veteran, still lives in Seward and doesn't consider himself a hero. But his record of six Mount Marathon wins is still remembered and celebrated in the mountain running community.

The Race Grows: 1946–61

From 1915 to 1950, only three to eight competitors entered the race each year, and the winners all lived in Seward at the time they won the race. Don Stickman of Ruby, Alaska, who won in 1951–52, was the first man to break the pattern. More changes were on the way when an international Olympic athlete competed and won in 1954. The first Olympic cross-country skier to make a name for himself on Mount Marathon was Sven Johansson. He arrived in the United States in 1951 after a successful sports career in his native Sweden.

After becoming a US citizen, Johansson won the North American Cross-Country Ski championship in 1955 and was a member of the 1960 US Olympic Cross-Country Ski Team. He trained with the US Biathlon Team at Fort Richardson in Anchorage, and was the first, but not the last, Mount Marathon winner to advocate running mountains to help build the speed and endurance needed for cross-country ski competitions.

So when a skiing buddy told Johansson about Seward's Fourth of July race, he decided to give it a try in 1952. Although Johansson finished fourth in his first attempt, he returned year after year to take part in the run, finishing second in 1953 and winning in 1954. Three years later, in 1957, he broke Ephraim Kalmakoff's long-standing record when he crossed the finish line in 51:40.

The Seward race day crowd burst into cheers as the big Swede ran across the finish line and into the record books in 1959. He'd run a per-

---

★ **1959: Alaska becomes the Forty-ninth State** ★

"We're In," shouted the headlines of the *Anchorage Daily Times* on June 30, 1958. The Statehood Act was passed in Congress and Alaska became the forty-ninth state in the union on January 3, 1959.

sonal best in 50:48, and his sixth-consecutive Mount Marathon win. Very little money changed hands on side bets that day because Johansson was the odds-on favorite to win.

As an Olympic "amateur athlete," Johansson refused prize money and donated his winnings to charity. By 1960 the race committee discontinued cash prizes to ensure that athletes could maintain their amateur status. Prize money was gone and race competitors ran for honor, glory, trophies, and medals. Johansson coached and taught skiing for twenty-five years in Alaska and was the first Alaskan to be named to the US Ski Hall of Fame.

Eberhard's team members (in the back row from the left) Chris Haines, Ed Schuser, Gene Morgan, Lewis Haines (grandfather of Kikkan Randall), and (in front) Stacy Taniguchi.

Race Participation Expands

1962–73

Year	Name	Time	Year	Name	Time
1962	Karl Bohlin	52:33	1968	Jonathan Chaffee	44:25 R
1963	Karl Bohlin	48:37 R	1969	Tom Besh	46:36
1964	Captain William Spencer	46:55 R	1970	Dale Shea	46:57
1965	Ed Williams	49:05	1971	Terry Aldrich	48:10
1966	Captain William Spencer	48:21	1972	Gene Morgan	46:16
1967	Jonathan Chaffee	44:28 R	1973	Tom Besh	45:49

The number of competitors continued to grow from sixty-three in 1950 to two hundred in 1983. Many factors contributed to the growing popularity of the race: team competition, significant advances in technique and training, the entrance of women and junior racers, and growth in media coverage.

Team competition was introduced in the '60s. Army and Air Force teams competed against each other and against civilian teams. The total times of a team's first four finishers were tallied to determine the winning team. Local athletes from around the state formed teams with colorful names like Arctic Air Burners, Mountain Goats, and the Alaska Streaking Team.

The Seward Mount Marathon Team won the nonmilitary class in 1963. They agonized about whether or not to compete after the death of their young captain, Dennis Hitt, who fell on a training run on nearby Mount Alice. The team decided to go ahead and compete as a way to honor Hitt's love of mountains and competitions. David Johnson, of the

Mountaineering Club of Alaska, took Hitt's place on the team and wore his uniform as a memorial tribute.

The First Women in the Race

A few days before the 1963 Mount Marathon run, three young women from Seward signed up for the race. Although race officials were against the idea, there were no rules prohibiting women from the competition.

According to Ann Wemark and Madeline Hicklin, it was all Jane Trigg's idea. It seems that Trigg had a crush on Karl Bohlin, the first man to run a sub-fifty-minute mile, and she figured the best place to get his attention was on a training run on Mount Marathon. Trigg—a local beauty and runner-up in the Miss Seward competition—and her friends

---

★ Mary Lowell ★

Thousands of years before the Russians sailed into Resurrection Bay, the Chugach people, along with Aleuts and Eskimos, used the area for trading and hunting expeditions. In 1792, the Native peoples abandoned the area after Baranov, the Russian governor of Alaska, built a fort in one of the coves dotting the bay and set up a shipbuilding facility. The Russians left the bay almost a hundred years later in 1867, when Russian Alaska became a territory of the United States.

One of the first women known to hike up Mount Marathon was Mary Lowell. In 1884, Mary was living on her husband's schooner and was about to have a baby. When they sailed into Resurrection Bay, she refused to sail any farther. Frank Lowell recognized a rebellion when he saw one and dropped anchor. They rowed ashore and built a home in the dense forest near the Mount Marathon trailhead. Mary Lowell picked berries and hunted ptarmigan on the lower slopes of the future race course. After her husband went back to sea in 1893, leaving Mary and their nine children, she filed for divorce and then filed on a homestead. She retained thirty-seven city lots when her homestead was purchased for the site of the new city of Seward on August 12, 1903. Every racer who competes in the Fourth of July race crosses part of the original Lowell Homestead.

worked the night shift at the shrimp cannery and trained in the morning after getting off from work.

The three young women were schoolmates who had just graduated that spring from Seward High School. All three had lived at the Jesse Lee Home during their high school years.

The young women talked to an *Anchorage Daily News* reporter before their inaugural run. Trigg reminisced about her first trip up the mountain: "It gave me great satisfaction, but I was tired." When asked about prerace "butterflies," she replied, "They're more like worms." Trigg's parents lived in Nome and didn't know that their daughter was planning to

Top: Jane Trigg won the first woman's race in 1:37:00, beating a few men in 1963.

Bottom from left: Madeline Hicklin, Jane Trigg, and Ann Wemark. The first three women to run the Mount Marathon Race in 1963, ten years before women were allowed to run in the Boston Marathon or the Dipsea Race.

run the race. Wemark's parents, who lived in Seward, echoed the sentiments of many folks in town, saying, "The girls must be crazy." Hicklin's parents were more supportive: "I think they're kind of tickled. I hope."

Jesse Lee Home students and teachers came out in force to cheer the women as they ran up the street with elite runners from the Army and Air Force biathlon teams. Trigg won the first women's race in 1:37:00, beating a few men, followed by Hicklin one minute later. Although Wemark came in dead last, half an hour later, the Seward crowd gave her a rousing welcome.

None of the women ran the race again, and Trigg's hoped-for romance with Bohlin never happened, but the trio did open the door for women to compete in the race.

The 1964 Earthquake

On March 27, 1964, a massive earthquake lasting more than five minutes with a magnitude of 9.2 on the Richter scale hit Prince William Sound. More than 115 people lost their lives statewide, and many coastal villages and towns were devastated.

Dale Shea, of Seward, who would go on to win the first junior race that year, was watching television when the first shock wave struck. He jumped to his feet, thinking that Seward was under attack. Shea explained, "With all the talk about the cold war I thought a bomb had exploded. Then Dad yelled, 'Earthquake!' and we ran outside and jumped into the car. Flames and smoke were shooting into the air from the ruptured fuel tanks at the harbor, and fire, fueled by gasoline, spread across the water. Our car joined a caravan of vehicles heading north. But we could only get three miles from town because the Resurrection Creek Bridge was twisted out of shape. We abandoned the car and walked across the debris where a family friend met us and drove us to his house."

The worst destruction was yet to come in the form of a forty-foot tsunami wave that slammed Seward twenty-six minutes after the first shock waves were felt. The monster wave picked up boats, houses, and railroad cars and scattered them helter-skelter. Twelve people died, six of them at the small boat harbor. Although Seward's economy, based on waterfront activities, was destroyed, within twenty-three hours, men and women were cleaning up the rubble. Without a working sewer system people went back to a more primitive way of getting rid of human waste. Shea smiled and said, "I got a job emptying honey buckets for $3.50 an hour. That was a lot of money for a kid in those days."

Twenty-six minutes after the first shock waves from the 1964 Good Friday Earthquake hit, a forty-foot tsunami wave slammed Seward. It picked up boats, houses, and railroad cars and scattered them like toys.

Although Seward residents were still recovering from the earthquake, town fathers decided to go ahead with the Mount Marathon Race. They hoped that the traditional Independence Day celebration would help bring normalcy to the town. The bridge had been fixed and the road was opened, at least some of the time. The roadbed had sunk in the quake and was covered with water at high tide.

A new race category was initiated in 1964 that allowed junior men and women ages fifteen to eighteen to compete if they were enrolled in high school, a member of a running team, and could pass a physical. Juniors raced to a point halfway up the mountain and back.

Dale Shea, a member of the Seward High School field and track, cross-country ski, and basketball teams, was eager to compete. He trained for the inaugural junior race with Mike Blatchford. "Blatchford's times were faster in training. I thought he would win," Shea commented, "but I jumped on my butt at the summit and slid for the first three hundred feet on the snow and was able to pull ahead, even though my glasses got covered in ice and snow crystals bruised my seat as my shorts rolled up." Shea made history when he won the first junior race in 28:28.

1970 was another big year for Shea. "I was in the best shape of my life," he reminisced in 2007. He ran track at Central Washington State College and had placed sixth in the 3,000-meter steeple-chase race sponsored by the National Association of Intercollegiate Associations (NAIA) and was eager to test himself against elite biathletes. Although he'd never run the full course in less than fifty minutes, he bounded ahead of the pack on the down trail to win in 46:57. "Measuring it against the highs I've enjoyed in life, it was a 'peak' experience," Shea said.

Seward had a new hero. Shea was the first hometown man to win the race since Hatch's victory in 1953, and he remains the only man born in Seward to win the adult—or senior—division of the men's race.

Race Participation Expands

Dale Shea (second row, fifth from the right) won the first junior race in 1964.

Captain William Spencer (front row, fifth from the left) and Sven Johansson (front row, second from the right) were members of the US Army Biathlon Team and Mount Marathon winners. Johansson was the first Mount Marathon winner to advocate running mountains to build speed and endurance for cross-country ski races.

Record Runners

Top Record Setters

Course records dropped faster than an anchor through water as well-trained amateur athletes entered the competition.

Team competition overshadowed solo runners for the next few years, but two Army biathlon team members set impressive records. Karl Bohlin was the first man to break the fifty-minute mark in 1963 when he crossed the finish line in 48:37.

Captain William Spencer: First to Break Forty-seven Minutes

One year later, Captain William Spencer, Bohlin's teammate, ran the second sub-fifty-minute Mount Marathon Race and beat Bohlin's record by almost two minutes with his finish in 46:55. After catching his breath at the finish line Spencer looked back at the mountain. "It's one of the best challenges around."

After finishing third one year earlier in 1963, Spencer set his sights on the gold. "Sven Johansson encouraged the biathletes to run in local races to stay in shape for the ski season. I worked Johansson's rigorous training schedule and was eager to test myself on Mount Marathon again."

But not all the excitement and drama associated with the race takes place on the slopes of Mount Marathon. Family members deal with unusual challenges too. After the awards ceremony, Spencer and his family piled into their Volkswagen camper and headed back to Anchorage. When they arrived at Summit Lake, halfway home, an exhausted Spencer decided to pull over and park for the night. His wife, Judy, eight and a half months pregnant, had arrived in Alaska one week earlier. She kept her

Captain William Spencer sprints down Fourth Avenue to set a new course record in 1964.

thoughts to herself as she tucked their eighteen-month-old son under a mound of blankets. After a restless night Judy woke in the morning to find water frozen in the sink. Hugging a blanket around her shoulders, she took a stand. "I'm not willing to camp with babies where water freezes in July." Two weeks later Judy gave birth to the first Spencer daughter and true to her word, never got into the VW camper for an overnight trip again.

Spencer didn't run the mountain in 1965 due to a sprained ankle. But the next year Judy agreed to another camping excursion after they bought a self-contained camper with a heater. With his family warm and happy, a relaxed Spencer won his second Mount Marathon Race in 48:21.

The Spencers had another surprise after the race. Judy remembers a man approaching her husband after the run. "He told Bill he'd given him the scare of his life when he saw us walk into the restaurant for breakfast that morning, trailed by three small children. He figured Bill probably hadn't slept a wink the night before. Turned out he'd bet a huge amount of money on Bill winning the race and thought he was going to lose his shirt. Bill and I really hadn't been aware of betting going on, but it helped explain the many pats on the shoulder, slaps on the back, and 'Thanks!'"

It was while working on a Boy Scout cross-country ski badge in Salt Lake City that Spencer fell in love with skiing. He skied competitively during high school and college before becoming a career military man. Spencer spent most of his adult life as a member of a biathlon team, a biathlon coach, and after retirement, as an Olympic biathlon official. He considers helping to design the Lake Placid Olympic biathlon course as one of his most satisfying accomplishments. His ever faithful wife, Judy, headed up a team of five hundred volunteers at the same Olympics.

Ten Top Women's and Men's Finishes on Mount Marathon

Men				Women		
1. Bill Spencer	00:43:21	1981		1. Nancy Pease	00:50:30	1990
2. Tobias Schwoerer	00:43:39	2004		2. Carmen Young-Dunham	00:50:54	1986
3. Trond Flagstad	00:44:03	2008		3. Nancy Pease	00:51:13	1989
4. Matt Novakovich	00:44:07	2012		4. Nancy Pease	00:51:41	1992
5. Bill Spencer	00:44:11	1974		5. Cedar Bourgeois	00:51:44	2005
6. Jonathan Chaffee	00:44:25	1968		6. Cedar Bourgeois	00:51:48	2010
7. Bill Spencer	00:44:25	1976		7. Holly Brooks	00:51:53	2012
8. Trond Flagstad	00:44:26	2012		8. Holly Brooks	00:51:58	2010
9. Bill Spencer	00:44:37	1975		9. Kikkan Randall	00:52:03	2011
10. Trond Flagstad	00:44:40	2008		10. Cedar Bourgeois	00:52:11	2008

Bill Spencer: King of the Mountain

In 1981, Bill Spencer (no relation to Captain William Spencer) became the first man to run a sub-forty-four-minute Mount Marathon Race. He also set the course record in both the junior and senior races and holds the record for most wins—eight—in the men's senior race.

Fellow athletes expound different theories to explain Spencer's running prowess. "Spencer is a human who has the attributes of a deer, to move fast and gracefully," says Sam Young, friend and fellow racer. Other runners point out that Spencer has the perfect body type for climbing mountains: strong legs, small build, and low body fat. Others agree, but add that it's his fierce competitive heart that's propelled him to eight wins on Mount Marathon.

The seeds to Spencer's phenomenal Mount Marathon career were planted when he was a teenager. His dad and three siblings all ran the race. "The race has always intrigued me," said Spencer. "I like the history behind it and the whole atmosphere on the Fourth of July." He ran his first Mount Marathon Race at age fifteen in 1971, placing third in the junior division. A year later he won, and in 1973 he set a new junior course record in 24:34.

"One year snow covered the ground from the halfway point to the bottom of the chute, and a few of us junior racers sewed leather on the back of our shorts and slid down the snow on our seats," Spencer recalled. "It was quite a ride."

When asked how he trained for his record-winning run, Spencer replied, "I was focused as a junior athlete, very self-motivated. My sister Lynn and I went to Seward for two weeks before the race and ran the junior race course twice a day," he said. "I've learned a few things about training since then, especially the benefits of tapering." Research indicates that runners need to cut back on their training a week or more prior to a race to give their bodies time to recover and refuel for a peak performance.

Spencer and his siblings' love of the outdoors and skiing were nurtured by his family on their homestead near Kenai, Alaska. His dad, a federal refuge supervisor for the Kenai National Moose Range, had skied for Penn State, and introduced his children to cross-country and alpine skiing at an early age. On weekends the whole family would drive to Turnagain Pass to cross-country ski, and they planned their vacations at Hatcher Pass, a ski area outside of Palmer, Alaska. Spencer gives his mother credit for keeping them healthy. He explained, "My mom was into nutrition long before anybody else."

Talented in both cross-country and alpine skiing, Spencer made the Junior Nationals for both sports in 1974. After much soul searching he chose to train with the cross-country ski team at Alaska Methodist University. After a winter of intense ski workouts he felt strong enough to go for a course record in his first Senior Mount Marathon Race. He was eighteen years old, five feet four inches tall, and weighed 100 pounds.

Spencer pulled away from the other racers on the uphill climb, reaching the top in 34:11. He remembers his feet lightly touching the surface of the rocks on the descent. The transition from downhill to street running is a critical time for competitors. Their legs are filled with lactic acid, wobbly and unresponsive. But Spencer had another worry. Spasms of pain gripped his side. As the roar of the crowd built in intensity, the pain quieted down, and Spencer was able to keep up his record-breaking pace. Spectators looked in awe at the official race clock as Spencer crossed the finish line in 44:11. He made it from the summit to the finish line in ten minutes.

Bill Spencer still holds course records in both the junior and senior races.

For the next twenty years Spencer skied in Olympic competitions, coached winning ski teams, earned two college degrees, and set course records in mountain runs.

The spillover from training at the national level in competitive ski racing propelled Spencer to three more Mount Marathon wins in 1981, 1982, and 1983. Most people assumed Mount Marathon couldn't be run in under forty-four minutes, but Spencer turned skeptics into believers in 1981 when he crossed the finish line in 43:21. "The media hype before each Mount Marathon Race was stressful, but I tried to run my own race," he said.

Between 1978 and 1994, Spencer was also a member of three National Cross-Country Olympic Ski Teams, and in 1985 he was the US National Cross-Country Ski champion. By 1989 Spencer was back in school at the

University of Vermont where he put on a coach's hat again and took the women's cross-country ski team to a national championship.

In 1991 Spencer returned to Alaska to take the job of assistant cross-country ski coach for the University of Alaska. After leaving competitive ski racing three years earlier, Spencer was invited to ski on the National Olympic Ski Team in 1994. At the end of the racing season he retired from competitive skiing for the second time.

While competing in Russia in 1989 Spencer met his future wife, Wendy, who also skied at the Olympic level for years. It's no surprise that Spencer would marry a woman who loved sports and mountains. After the birth of their three children, Anne, David, and Nowelle, Spencer's main focus is now on family activities. He and Wendy enjoy recreational sports that all the family can participate in: hiking, biking, and orienteering.

The love of running appears to be genetic in the Spencer family. In 2006 Spencer's eleven-year-old daughter, Anne, asked her dad if she could run the Junior Mount Marathon Race. He said, "If that's what you want to do, I'll help you train for the race."

Since the combined junior girls and boys race is limited to two hundred runners, any girl or boy wanting to get into the race must put their name into a lottery. When Anne's name wasn't picked in the lottery and she couldn't run, she begged her dad to run in her place. (Any past Mount Marathon winner can pick up a bib the night before the race.) Spencer didn't want to disappoint his daughter so he returned to the race in 2006. Anne found a way for the whole family to be involved. She went to the halfway point with her violin so she could play for her dad as he ran by. Her aunt, Lynn Spencer (Spencer's sister and three-time Olympic competitor), hiked up the mountain with six-year-old David so that David could make a "GO DADDY" message with small rocks for his dad to see as he neared the summit. Wife Wendy brought up the rear with their youngest daughter, Nowelle, in a backpack, to cheer for Spencer on his way down the mountain.

Spencer was the sixty-fifth finisher in the men's race to cross the finish line in 2006, totally at peace with his time, perfectly satisfied to just "be there and be part of the experience."

One year later in 2006, Anne's name was picked in the lottery and she ran the junior race for the first time, wearing the T-shirt her father wore when he set his first record in 1973.

In 2012 all three Spencer children ran the junior race. Ann, now seventeen, came in second for the girls, eleven-year-old David finished fifth in the boys division, and ten-year-old Nowelle Spencer placed thirty-third in the junior girl's race. It appears that the Spencer children have inherited their dad's competitive spirit and take to mountain running like ducks to water.

Eric Strable, 2011 Men's Winner

If at first you don't succeed, train smarter. That's Eric Stable's race strategy. For years his dream was to win the Mount Marathon Race. Although he'd won a fistful of silver and bronze metals with five top three finishes, gold eluded him. Then in 2011, on his twelfth quest, he won the race in 44:40. Not only was he first across the finish line, but he ran a sub-forty-five minute race, becoming one of only eight men to finish in under forty-five minutes. Ever. And against all odds, Eric's finish time was exactly the same as Trond Flagstad in 2010, resulting in a tie for ninth fastest run. Sweeter yet, it propelled Eric into the elite top ten Mount Marathon bracket, proving his race strategy worked.

Eric didn't increase training hours in 2011, but focused on mountain runs. In the three months leading up to the race, Eric ran 150,000 vertical feet up mountains, and then down again. The equivalent of seven runs to the summit of Mount McKinley, North America's highest mountain. "I ran downhill as fast as I could but wasn't out of control," he said. He does, however, admit, that "Everyone has a different idea about what constitutes out of control."

The hours of downhill training paid off for Eric in an unbelievable

10:25 sprint from the summit to the finish line, a little over a mile and a half. Second-place finisher Brent Knight reached the summit almost a minute ahead of Eric's 34:15. But Eric attacked the downhill section like a man possessed, ate up Brent's lead, catapulted past him, and crossed the finish line first. Brent Knight's downhill run of 11:45 was exceptional, but Eric's run seized the day.

With Eric's parents, both marathon runners, as role models, he began running and skiing competitively in elementary school. "I've always liked being active. I like to push myself to be the best I can be as an athlete." During his years at Colony High in Palmer, Eric was a star runner and skier.

Besides the intrinsic rewards of competition, his athletic achievements paid off financially. Eric won a scholarship in running and skiing to the University of Alaska Anchorage, where he was an NCAA All-American skier. He also placed in the top ten at the World Junior Championships.

After graduating with a degree in engineering in 2005 Eric worked as an engineer for two years and retired from skiing competition. "I just got lazy for a while. But I missed being competitive and started entering road races. Running is easy; I don't need equipment and usually train alone. I consider myself a recreational, competitive runner." His 2006 record-breaking Crow Pass run in 3:05:00 tells a different story. Recreational run it is not. The twenty-four-mile race course over a mountain pass, through a river, across rocks, roots, and snow, tests top runners in the field. Although Eric's record was broken in 2009 by current record holder Geoff Roes, who finished in 2:57:11, Eric came in a close second in 2:58:30. Geoff and Eric are the only men to run the Crow Pass Race in under three hours, the equivalent of running a four-minute mile.

Eric coached the UAA Ski Team for two seasons, 2004 and 2006, and realized he liked the job. His passion for coaching led him to accept the position of head junior coach at Alaska Pacific Nordic Ski Training Center in Anchorage. "I wanted to share what I'd learned with young talented skiers. I want to engineer skiers to be the fastest in the world through education and empowerment."

After the 2011 mountain running season was over, Eric began to train for his first fifty-mile race. But come springtime Eric will be back in the mountains, "I have to defend my Mount Marathon title," he says. "There are many hungry runners out there who'd love to beat my time."

Now that he's revealed the secret of his success, Eric may have a lot of company on those downhill mountain runs. But, then again, maybe Eric will come up with a new strategy for next year.

Although Strable didn't hold on to his title in 2012, he posted the fastest downhill time in an unbelievable 10:08.

Nancy Pease: Women's Record Holder

Poetry in motion is how many fans describe Nancy Pease, women's record holder. Her fearless, competitive spirit lay hidden beneath a petite physique and sunny smile.

After Pease's record run in 1989 when she placed fourth overall on Mount Marathon, she explained why she likes running with men: "The race is a great equalizer. It would be a thrill to think that my best would be the winning time, overall, on Mount Marathon." Her finish in 51:13 was a mere two minutes off Mike Graham's winning run of 49:16.

"If you want to draw out the best inside, there's nothing like pressure. I like running with the men because they pull me along and add to the challenge," she said.

Pleased with her fifth-place finish overall in 1990 in 50:30, Pease grew pensive. "I think women can go under fifty minutes, and I think that race is still ahead of me." Three years later, that race was within her grasp.

"I was in the best shape of my life in 1993," said Pease, who had trained for a sub-fifty-minute run on Mount Marathon. Three weeks before the Fourth of July race, Pease was first overall (man or woman) to reach the top of Bird Ridge, an arduous three-mile mountain climb, in 43:00. Mountain runners like to point out that a runner's finish time in the Bird Ridge race is usually equal to their finish in the Mount Marathon Race.

Even though Pease had trained diligently, she suffered from prerace jitters. "My personal goals and the media buildup are stressful. And flitting on the border between speed and danger is also a worry. One false step puts the fear in you: you tighten up and slow down. A few days before the Mount Marathon Race I had recurrent nightmares about not being prepared, that I'd be standing at the starting line like the emperor with no clothes."

On July third, the night before the race, Pease went out to eat with her husband for a meal of mussels. Within hours she got violently sick and couldn't run on the Fourth. "I suffered from P.T.S, post-traumatic [Mount Marathon] stress syndrome. I often wonder what might have been. You only get one chance at the perfect race, and that was supposed to be mine."

Nancy Pease set the course record for women in 1990.

The journey from casual to elite athlete began for Pease as a kid when she tagged along with her dad on runs. By sixth grade she started to practice for running events, and by junior and senior high school she was training seriously. Like many Mount Marathon champions, Pease skied competitively during the winter months. Tom Corbin, her high school coach, took the team into the mountains on training runs during the summer as part of their cross training for skiing. Pease found solace and renewal on these outings: "It gave me a reason to be in the mountains in spring, to be rejuvenated by sunlight, flowers, and breathtaking views."

After a successful cross-country skiing career in high school, culminating in placing second in state, Pease set her sights on college competition. She remembers how hard it was, the extra level of discipline she needed to keep her body fat ratio low. She was a petite 5 feet, 4 inches and weighed 96 pounds when she set off for college and four more years of ski competition at Dartmouth. By now physical activity was an ingrained habit.

One of Pease's summer activities was to run the Crow Pass Crossing Race, in which she was the women's winner the nine times she entered. Her personal best finish on the twenty-six-mile mountain run, which includes a glacial stream crossing, was 3:26:00. "I do it because of the beautiful Alaskan setting, and because I enjoy the training and being part of physically fit friends," she said. She credits Bill Spencer and Tim Neale, two of her training partners, for helping her build strength as a competitor: "They pulled me along, made me stronger."

After marriage and the birth of two sons, Pease changed her focus to her family. "I do miss competitions, but my philosophy of life has changed. I still run five times a week, but now I look on it as a way to energize myself and to stay fit."

Pease can look back at her running achievements with pride. She holds the Mount Marathon Race women's course record, and the third- and fourth-fastest women's finish times.

"The challenge is still out there to perform at an elite level," said Pease. "I'm not quite finished yet."

Tobias Schwoerer: The Contender

Rumors that a new competitor was going for a record swept through the Fourth of July crowd in 2004. "Who's the new guy?" "Don't know." "I hear he's going for a record." Most people on the street had never heard of Tobias Schwoerer, but that was about to change.

> ### ★ The Lottery ★
>
> As the race grew in popularity, it was necessary to limit the number of runners to protect the mountain environment. Any runner who finishes the race is eligible to return again the next year. Since 85 percent of competitors return each year, and more runners want into the race than there are slots available, a new runner must put his or her name into the lottery in hopes of getting a bib. Until a later ruling allowed elite runners to compete, the only other option was to bid on one of the ten available bibs at the auction held the night before the race.

When Schwoerer burst from the cliff at the base of the mountain the crowd checked their watches and roared their approval. The cheers along the street grew in intensity as Schwoerer sprinted down Fourth Avenue and across the finish line in 43:39, the second man to run a sub-forty-four-minute race.

After his amazing run, Schwoerer commented, "It's totally unique, a real Alaskan thing to do. It's crazy and dangerous, like a drug. When I tell friends in Germany that people pay over one thousand dollars to buy their way into the race, they shake their heads in disbelief.

"As a kid growing up in Germany I was fascinated with the idea of coming to Alaska. I read everything I could about the Russian explorers and fur traders in Alaska and I pored over Alaskan photography books."

It was Schwoerer's athletic talent that brought him to Alaska in 2000. A family friend hooked him up with Bill Spencer, ski coach at the University of Alaska, and Spencer helped him get a skiing and running scholarship at the University of Alaska Anchorage. It was a good fit for both Schwoerer and the university. With the help of Schwoerer's running strength, the UAA cross-country running team took its first trip to the NCAA Division II Regional Championships, where Schwoerer placed second. He and teammate Eric Strabel, who finished fifteenth, both garnered All Region honors. "I made many new friends on the running and ski teams. For me, I love to be outside with friends, the endorphins flow and I feel so good."

During the three years that Schwoerer skied and ran for the UAA Seawolves, he became the first to earn All-American honors in both sports. He was also named UAA Athlete of the Year in 2001–2 and received the Team Scholar-Athlete award for his 3.94 overall GPA in economics.

Recognizing Schwoerer's athletic prowess, and thinking that he might have a shot at a Mount Marathon record, Eric Strabel and Bill Spencer urged Schwoerer to enter the race. But there was a problem. "I actually never thought I would have a chance to run this race," Schwoerer said. "It's almost impossible for a new runner to get into the race."

The door opened for elite runners to get a bib in 2003 when Fred Moore spearheaded a rule change that allowed elite athletes into the race. The new rule stated that the winner of any of the seven Alaskan Mountain Running Grand Prix races is eligible to get a bib for the Mount Marathon Race.

Schwoerer's win in the Bird Ridge Race in June 2004 made him eligible to run Mount Marathon a month later. "It's really important to have that rule in place," Schwoerer said. "Mount Marathon is not just a wilderness run. There's a lot of technical stuff. It requires specific preparations. I trained at top speed on the lower part in the chute, which requires the most technical skill." Schwoerer added, "I felt a lot of pressure on race day and hadn't slept well the night before. I stayed out of sight until the start. Aaron Dickson, a friend and fellow UAA runner, and

Toby Schwoerer, second man to run a sub-forty-four minute race.

I planned for Dickson to lead me out fast to the base of the mountain. I ran the race hard from the very beginning."

Schwoerer powered his way to the top in 32:30, before starting his descent. "At the cliffs I lost my balance and almost fell. By the time I reached the road my legs were so wobbly I could hardly control them. But by the time I neared the finish line I was feeling good and reached out to touch a couple of hands. I thought I was way under the record, but I'd looked at the wrong timing clock." Record or not, Schwoerer had a phenomenal run, the second fastest finish in race history, a mere eighteen seconds off Bill Spencer's record.

Schwoerer's sports career began in Germany and was nurtured by his family. "My dad competed in alpine skiing competitions when he was younger and he took the whole family alpine skiing on weekends. I started competing in ski races when I was twelve and spent five years on the German Junior National Ski Team."

In the fall of 2004 Schwoerer went to graduate school in British Columbia, earning a master's degree in environmental economics. Today Schwoerer considers himself a recreational athlete. He runs every morning before work, and sometimes adds another short run at lunchtime or in the evening. Schwoerer enjoys the camaraderie of friends on long weekend treks into the mountains. He'd like to write a book about back country adventures one day and he might coach. "It's time to give something back to the community," he said.

Trond Flagstad: Norwegian Transplant

In 2008, Trond Flagstad posted the third fastest run ever on Mount Marathon in 44:03. "It's an extremely unique race. There's nothing like it anywhere," he said. "I looked at the mountain and thought that it might be fun to give it a try." When he decided to enter the run a year later, his goal was to win. "I've been competitive all my life—I do a race to win," he said.

Flagstad, a native of Norway, was skiing at the age of three and cross-country skiing competitively by age ten. He represented Norway in World Cup cross-country ski races until he was twenty-nine.

He met his future wife, Lindsay, while visiting skiing buddies in Massachusetts in 1999, and a year later they came to Alaska. He got a job as the assistant ski coach at UAA and skis about two hours a day, six days a week, as part of his coaching duties, during the competitive ski season.

He'd never been up Mount Marathon before his first race in 2000, but he still finished in 47:06. Although Flagstad ran five consecutive Mount Marathon Races in less than fifty minutes, first place eluded him. From 2005–7, Flagstad crossed the finish line in second place: thirty-five seconds behind Brian Bethard in 2005, and twelve seconds behind Brad Precosky, in both 2006 and 2007. "You have to be hungry," he told an *Anchorage Daily News* reporter. "I've been second three years in a row. Second is good, but, if you're just happy with that, you'll never win. You have to think, 'Second is first loser.'"

Flagstad's goal of winning the race and setting an age group record was supported by his family. Lindsay prepared healthy, low-fat meals, and didn't bring junk food in the house, while his ten-month-old son, twenty-two-pound Vebjorn, helped his dad build strength by riding along in a backpack when his dad did hill work.

By race day, Flagstad, who stands five foot, eleven inches, at 165 pounds was 5 pounds lighter than the previous year. He increased his running miles and he and his wife ran the Boston Marathon in April 2008. After returning from Boston he increased his hill workouts. Training buddies Harlow Robinson and Barney Griffith did their bit by racing him up Flattop Mountain in the weeks prior to the race.

On race day, Flagstad was ready. He took off his watch so he couldn't put pressure on himself. Although he took off fast, Sam Hill and Brent Knight beat him to the base of the mountain. "I wanted to keep the two of them in sight," Flagstad said. "I caught Knight at the halfway point on the uphill trail, and could see Hill ahead of me. Hill reached the top almost a minute ahead of me, but I knew that downhill is my strength. I ran fast and jumped off the top of the mountain onto the snow." Flagstad slid down the snow on his back, legs extended in a luge position but without the luge. "The ride down was bumpy and I was afraid I'd get the wind knocked out of me. People who saw me said I was flying." When asked how he was able to stop his downward plunge he replied, "I watched the gravel by the side of the snow chute, and when I thought I was near the end, I dug in my heels and stood up. I caught up with Hill at the halfway point, on the downhill course, and picked up another minute in the waterfall descent, to finish almost two minutes ahead of him."

Flagstad went on to explain how he prepared for the snow. "I wore a singlet to protect my back and spandex shorts that went down to my knees. I practiced going down snow on the mountains around Anchorage, and went to Seward and spent three days practicing on the snow on Mount Marathon." His intense training schedule paid off. Flagstad made it from the summit to the finish line in an astonishing 10:15, matching Brad Precosky's run in 2001.

In 2008, Trond Flagstad posted the third fastest run on Mount Marathon.

As Flagstad crossed the finish line, a smile brightened his face and he pumped his fist into the air and shouted, "Finally!"

One characteristic of most Mount Marathon competitors is that they start planning for next year's run, within seconds after crossing the finish line. Flagstad is no exception. "I'd like to talk Toby Schwoerer, a friend of mine, into returning to the race next year. We could train for a record run together," he said.

Matt Novakovich: 2012 Men's Mount Marathon Winner Fourth Fastest Time

"There's no greater race in Alaska, the total environment: the police car leading you down Jefferson Street, the helicopter hovering overhead, and the shouts of encouragement from race fans," said Matt Novakovich, the 2012 Mount Marathon champion. He should know: he chalked up the fourth fastest finish in race history when he crossed the finish line in 44:07.

Raised in Anchorage, Novakovich started running track at Dimond High School, and went on to compete in steeplechase races at Brigham Young University. The need to be flexible was paramount because of the water crossings and hurdles. Novakovich felt his lack of flexibility was holding him back and he developed an improvement plan. He sat on the ground with one leg stretched in front and the other back with his knee bent for a half hour at a time while he studied. It paid off. He was able to use either leg to lead jumping over hurdles. This willingness to train for specific types of races would lead to his success a few years later on Mount Marathon.

After college Novakovich began cycling semiprofessionally and won the Tour of Anchorage, a cycling event, and set many uphill cycling race records.

In 2008 Novakovich was introduced to mountain running and he's never looked back. "Broken chains, flat tires, or gear problems can influence bike races. But mountain running is such a pure sport, human against the mountain. That's why I love it so much." Novakovich was given a slot to run in the 2009 Mount Marathon race after writing a letter seeking a special invitation into the race. His wife, Tiffany, also harbored Mount Marathon dreams and was able to buy a women's bib for $380. Both were ecstatic.

His first Mount Marathon race in 2009, when Novakovich finished tenth in 51:52, left him with a burning desire to run faster. And improve he did; in 2010 he finished in 48:35, and a year later he placed fifth overall in 46:44. Then he set his sights on winning.

But his dreams were put on hold after surgery to repair a torn meniscus in November 2011. Running downhill on his knee was out of the question. So in January 2012 he purchased a treadmill with the capacity of a 40 percent incline, installed it in his garage, and began daily workouts. A few days later, as he was running nine- to ten-minute intervals, at 40 percent grade, he smelled smoke; the circuit board was on fire. After the NordicTrack company replaced the circuit board and a few heat resistors, the company designed a new, more powerful machine. Novakovich likes to think that his persistence and advice helped NordicTrack design a better treadmill. Tiffany and children Josh and Liz also used the treadmill for training workouts.

Starting slowly, Novakovich worked up to running 25,000 vertical feet of treadmill workouts every week. "The treadmill has many advantages; I can watch a football game or babysit my youngest daughter, Sophie."

"At thirty-eight years old, I'm competing against better athletes, so I figured I would have to do more to beat them." In addition to treadmill workouts, Novakovich trained on Mount Marathon twenty times so that he knew the exact route he planned to traverse. His friend and fellow competitor Barney Griffith trained with him and gave him many helpful tips on the downhill section of the race.

Race day arrived with Novakovich hungry for a win. He pulled ahead of the elite group of runners some two hundred feet above the cliffs, near a landmark called the squirrel tree. But the speed of his uphill climb took its toll on his legs, and they were cramping severely by the time he reached the summit. Although he had run down the snow on training runs, he sat and slid down the snowfield to give his legs a rest and reduce his heart rate. "I felt like I was slowing down and worried that Trond Flagstad, who I knew could catch up on the downhill, was closing the gap.

"Then Jerry Ross, my friend and coach, whose job is to keep me focused, met me at the halfway point of the downhill section. He called out that I was doing fine and on track."

Near the cliffs Novakovich stumbled, and a fan helped calm him down when he called out, "Take a deep breath and relax."

Checking his watch, Novakovich saw that he'd reached his goal of forty minutes to the bottom of the cliff. "I might have a chance at the record," he mused, but when he reached Front Street his legs cramped again and he had to fight just to finish the race. "I was going to win or pass out trying," he said later, recalling the agony of the last few blocks. "I had to push through the pain."

His kids Josh and Liz ran the last few yards with him and were sobbing by the time he crossed the finish line.

Although he had just won the most coveted mountain race in Alaska, he was in pain and couldn't savor the victory. Only later, after he wobbled to the shower, did it sink in. The prize was his. "It's the best thing I've ever done," he said proudly.

During the 2012 Mount Marathon Race Matt Novakovich posted the fourth fastest run in race history.

The year 2012 was a banner year for the Novakovich family. Tiffany finished fifteenth in the women's race, and nine-year-old Liz and eleven-year-old Josh finished twenty-fifth and thirty-second in the junior race. In 2013 Novakovich's third child, Tali, will be seven years old on the Fourth of July, old enough to race in the juniors. Novakovich and his wife will wait until next year to see if Tali is ready. If so, they will train with her until they feel she knows the route down by heart. They use clues to help the children remember the route. At the top of the cliff area I tell them, "Turn right at the scarecrow tree." Only when they feel confident that the children are safe do they give their consent.

Novakavich set himself a new goal for 2013: he hopes to break Bill Spencer's race record set in 1981 in 43:21.

"I know it's possible because I ran the course forty-five seconds faster on a training run in 2012," said Novakovich. Since starting his mountain running career, Novakovich has lowered his weight from 175 to 165 pounds, and hopes to drop another few pounds before the 2013 race. Of course the real question on everyone's mind is, will the new, improved treadmill be able to handle Novakovich's more aggressive workout plans?

Jonathan Chaffee: Army Biathlon Team

Jonathan Chaffee was the first man to run a sub-forty-five minute race in 1967 in 44:28. Then he came back one year later and shaved three seconds off his record. Chaffee was a twenty-two-year-old Private First Class stationed at Fort Richardson and a member of the Army Biathlon Team when he made his historic runs.

When asked if he was stronger on the uphill or downhill section of the race, he said, "I was strong on both. I got up to the top in thirty minutes and down in fifteen. At the snow chute I sat down on my seat, flew down the snow, and shot out onto the shale and landed on my feet. It was an ecstatic experience that few other running events can duplicate." When asked how he became so fearless running down steep slopes, he responded, "I went with my dad, a paleontologist, to the Badlands for three different summers and while Dad hunted for fossils, I ran mountains."

Chaffee went on to comment about the Seward crowd. "The only other place I felt such energy from the crowd was when I crossed the finish line at the King's Cup cross-country ski race in Oslo, Norway, to the cheers from thirty thousand spectators. For fun and sheer exuberance you can't beat the Mount Marathon and King's Cup races. There's no better feeling in the world than being in a race when everything is going well." Another peak experience was Chaffee's participation in the Olympic Games in Grenoble, France. He also competed on two Olympic cross-country ski teams at the national and international levels. He reminisced, "I enjoyed competing at the elite level."

A gifted athlete, Chaffee first realized that he might have a natural ability to run in eighth grade. When the basketball team ran around the town square to build endurance, he always made it around before anyone else.

"Back in the days when New Hampshire was covered in snow from November to March, I spent hours cross-country skiing," he said. Like many Mount Marathon champions, Chaffee skied and ran and excelled in both.

The two years Chaffee was stationed in Anchorage, he won almost every marathon, 10K, and 5K road race he entered.

In the fall of 1968, after his discharge from the Army, he went back to college and graduated with a degree in cellular and developmental biology. After sustaining a sports injury competing in a race he hadn't trained for, Chaffee couldn't run for ten years without getting a headache. Today, he runs and skis two to three miles a day in the White Mountains in New Hampshire, savoring the sun and snow and thankful to be healthy and fit again. He still holds the record for the fourth and seventh fastest men's finishes in the Mount Marathon Race.

Carmen Young Dunham: Hometown Girl

Many Mount Marathon champions credit coaches and teammates for helping them reach their athletic goals. Seward-born Dunham, who ran the second fastest woman's finish in 50:54 in 1986, fought her way to victory without the benefit of either. Talent, grit, and determination propelled Dunham into the winner's circle. She reminisced, "I used to run everywhere as a kid. My three siblings and I spent hours outside every day exploring the Seward docks, beaches, and waterfront."

At the urging of her high school PE coach, the petite, athletic Dunham ran the Junior Mount Marathon Race twice, and then walked away from competition. In 1982—a decade later—at the age of twenty-seven she returned to the race and set her first record. "I didn't have a clue

In 2006 at age fifty-two Carmen Young-Dunham set a new record for her age group. Her 50:54 finish in 1986 remains the second fastest time among all women.

how to train for my first Senior Mount Marathon Race. I went up the mountain almost every day." She paused, the hint of a smile on her face. "If I knew then what I know now, I would have trained much differently. On the day of the race my knees were pretty wobbly by the time I got to the top. Then I saw that Karen Jeske's were wobbly too, so I went for it." Dunham won and Jeske placed second in 58:21.

From 1963 to 1985 men and women ran the Mount Marathon Race together. "For myself, I like a separate race for women. I can see my competition." When asked about her strategy for the race she said, "This race is about climbing; I tried to pull ahead on the uphill section. I'm not comfortable on the street portion of the course, but once I get to the mountain I feel better. I picked up time because of the big snowfield at the summit; the more snow, the faster my finish."

A shy, reserved woman, Dunham said that she breathed a sigh of relief when Nancy Pease broke her record in 1990 in 50:30. "It's kind of nice not to have the record anymore," she said. "Now people will be after Nancy instead of me." Dunham finished second in 52:58.

"My folks are my biggest fans. They were always happy to watch my kids while I trained and ran the race, and they always made it to the finish line to cheer me across," she said. Dunham is proud of her Native heritage: "My grandmother was Eskimo. But I never got to meet her because she died before I was born." Her ancestors were able to adapt and flourish in arctic Alaska, an environment most would call hostile.

Dunham's ability to stay competitive year after year in the difficult world of mountain running is a tribute to her hardy ancestors.

When asked about her strengths and weaknesses as a runner, Dunham replied, "When I was younger I was strong on both the uphill and downhill sections of the race. Now that I'm older, I'd say that downhill is my strength. I've done most of my training alone and it's been a lot of trial and error." She hesitated, looked out the window, before continuing. "I'm really bad about listening to my body; so consequently, I've suffered from shin splints, plantar fasciitis, and a torn meniscus."

When Carmen married Kevin Dunham her life had come full circle. She and Dunham were both born on the same day, in the same hospital in Seward and had gone to school together. After traveling in opposite directions for years they came together again in 2003.

Seward folks line the streets on race day to support hometown runners. In 2006 when fifty-two-year-old Dunham placed fifth in the women's race in 1:01:28 and set a new fifty to fifty-nine age group record, her friends and neighbors roared their approval. The thirty to thirty-nine age group record she set in 1986 in 50:30 has never been broken.

When asked how she manages to work mountain training into her busy schedule of work and family, she replied, "I really enjoy it and it makes me feel good."

Sam Young: From the Prairies to the Mountain

Sam Young's journey from prairie dweller to Mount Marathon champion, with his win in 1985 in 44:49, began after the family moved from Nebraska to Colorado. The Rocky Mountains, with their towering peaks, became an enormous playground for Young, who as a teenager set off on horseback, traveling over two hundred miles, on a solo camping trip into the mountains.

After returning home, he grew restless. "I was ready for a new adventure," he said. As he thumbed through an atlas, seeking a new direction, his finger tapped on Seward, Alaska. "I had a premonition that I'd live in

Alaska one day," he said. A year later he stood by the roadway, thumb in the air, heading north. Young arrived in Seward a few days before the 1975 Mount Marathon Race. The frontier atmosphere of the small town impressed him.

On the Fourth of July, Young watched Bill Spencer lope across the finish line in 44:37. A fire was ignited within Young. He wanted to be part of the race.

After working at Port Graham that summer, he headed back to Seward, where he was befriended by Blaine Barthanson. Barthanson loaned Young a tent and a woodstove, and let him camp on his beach property for the winter. Young spent the winter planning a trip around the world and the Mount Marathon Race was not on his schedule. Then, just three weeks before the Fourth of July, he changed his mind and started to train for the run.

On race day Young was in pain by the halfway point. Then Betsy Haines, a young woman with a big smile on her face, passed him. Now he was humbled and in pain. "I vowed that if I ever did the race again I'd be better prepared."

A few days later Young and his traveling companion set off on a trip round the world. "Climb every mountain" was their mantra. They started with 8,100-foot Mount Galdhøppigen, Norway's highest peak, then hiked the Khyber Pass in Afghanistan, the Himalayas in Nepal, and the Andes Mountains of Bolivia. When asked about his passion for mountain trails, Young replied, "Being in the mountains make me feel more grounded, connected with life. It's a privilege and a gift to be able to stand on a mountaintop."

Returning home, Young attended college and didn't come back to the race until 1979. After finishing tenth that year, Young remembers thinking, "If I train for this race, I just might be able to win it." He upped his training schedule and by the early '80s he was competing in 10K and mountain runs around the state. He set a record in the Pillar Mountain Run in Kodiak, Alaska, that stood until 2005.

Young trained hard for the 1984 Mount Marathon Race, and finished in 50:47. But he paid a price. The temperature was 85°F by the time the men's race started. Young didn't carry water and there was none on the course. "I was ready to pass out halfway down the mountain. I was just hanging on when I got to the street." Young managed to persevere until he crossed the finish line and then passed out. Friends pulled him over to the curb and hosed him down. Two hours later a spectator looked at Young, who lay unresponsive on the sidewalk, and commented, "He doesn't look too good." Helping hands picked Young up and took him to the hospital to be rehydrated. It took him six months to recuperate from the effects of the dehydration and the dollar-sized blisters on his heels. As soon as he felt strong again, Young started training for the 1985 race. Mountain runners seem to have an enhanced ability to forget pain and suffering.

Young fought hard and earned his win in the 1985 Mount Marathon Race, which turned into a duel between him and Bill Spencer. After trading the lead back and forth, Young remembers reaching the top first. "Then Spencer put on his skis and passed me on the snow. We traded the lead again. Spencer pulled passed me at the bottom of the chute and surged ahead. I lost sight of Spencer for a while and didn't know where he was. Then I spotted him near the hospital. I gradually gained on Spencer and by the time we reached Fourth Avenue we were running side by side."

The deafening cheers from the Seward crowd helped propel Young forward and across the finish line eighteen seconds ahead of Spencer. Young reached out to clasp Spencer's hand. "Thanks for pulling and pushing me along."

Young's goal in 1986 was to win his third consecutive Mount Marathon Race, and the perpetual trophy given to three-time consecutive winners. Young had started a new business and was a stay-at-home dad. He set high goals for himself: the summit in thirty-three minutes, down to midpoint in four minutes, four minutes to the bottom of the chute, and

Sam Young won his third consecutive race in 1986 when he and Bill Spencer crossed the finish line together—the only tie in race history.

four minutes to the finish line. He recalled, "I was a fast runner in those days."

"During the 1986 Mount Marathon Race, music swirled through my head as I dueled with Bill Spencer for the lead. The theme song from *Chariots of Fire* propelled me up the street. Once we reached the base of the mountain the music changed. I had just seen the movie *Deliverance* and the guitar strains of "Dueling Banjos" began, and ebbed and swelled in my head as Spencer and I swapped leads. First Spencer gave his all and passed me at the halfway point. Then it was my turn to show off my climbing skills, and I passed Spencer near the top. Spencer replied with a daring pass near the halfway point on the downhill section. Then I edged by Spencer in the waterfall. Spencer, feet flying like fingers dancing across banjo strings, jumped ahead. Music subsides, builds in intensity, propelling me past Spencer again a half mile from the finish line. The Seward crowd went crazy when Spencer caught up with me at Fourth and Jefferson. Twenty feet from the finish line Spencer turned to me, 'Do you want to tie the race?' I had to catch my breath. 'Yeah.' Thundering chords of *Chariots of Fire* crescendo; we clasped hands and crossed the finish line together in a time of 45:32." The duel ended in a standoff. It was the first and only time the Mount Marathon Race has ended in a tie.

After the 1986 Mount Marathon Race, Young ran recreationally and focused on family and community activities. He worked many years with junior runners as part of Seward's Parks and Recreation program, by taking kids up Mount Marathon on training runs.

Young and his wife, Bonnie, both certified yoga instructors, are involved in the Healthy Futures program, promoting fitness activities for elementary students. They were married on the Fourth of July in 2002, eloping to a scenic viewpoint a few miles north of Seward, between the men's and women's race. He added, "I wanted to be married on a day that was easy to remember."

As a recreational athlete, Young sums up his philosophy of life. "It's not how far or how fast you run, but how often. Your body is a gift to be treasured and taken care of."

Cedar Bourgeois: Late Bloomer

Cedar Bourgeois, a reserved and feminine young woman, has won the Mount Marathon Race five times and holds four of the top ten finishes. She appears almost fragile as she walks around her hometown of Seward with her children Zen and Coral. But beneath the shyness and flowing skirts beats the heart of a world-class athlete.

Bourgeois joins a distinguished group of Seward competitors who have won the Mount Marathon Race. Many people ask, "How can this tiny community produce so many outstanding athletes?" The most common answer is, "Location, location, location." Mount Marathon is an accessible playground for local athletes.

Although Bourgeois took part in sports in high school, she did not have a passion for them. After graduating from Seward High School, marriage and motherhood became Bourgeois's priority for the next decade. Her journey from chasing toddlers to chasing records began in 1997. After finishing third, five minutes behind Nina Kemppel, Olympic skier and owner of nine Mount Marathon first-place medals, Bourgeois looked at her own performance and said, "I can do better." She was quick to add that she wasn't trying to beat Kemppel or anyone else, but to set a new goal for herself. Bourgeois had discovered her passion: she loved the thrill of competition. "Mountain running has shaped my character as a woman," she told a *Mount Marathon Magazine* reporter in 2008.

With each mountain practice or competitive run, Bourgeois repeats the same phrase in her head, "Never let other people tell you what you can or can't do." It makes one wonder who told Bourgeois she couldn't run down Mount Marathon faster in 2005 than she did in 2004. She floated over and on top of shale, rocks, and water on her descent from the top to the base, achieving a personal best finish and a win in 51: 44.

Cedar Bourgeois, winner of four races, holds four of the top ten finish records.

"I studied the mountain a lot more," she said, "And knew where to put my feet on the downhill section of the run." Bourgeois, twenty-nine, ran almost four minutes faster than she did one year earlier. "I felt better, a lot more familiar with the mountain," she commented after the race. When asked what advice she had for new runners, she said, "Never put constraints on yourself."

She power walks, runs trails, and climbs mountains five days a week year-round. Around the first of April to the Fourth of July race, she climbs Mount Marathon twice a week, and does interval workouts during trail runs. Even a leisurely training run can leave her body bloody and bruised. Bourgeois still cringes when she recalls the tumble she took while running down the snowfield near the summit. She suddenly dropped six feet through the soft snow and ended up with a frozen backside and bloody legs.

Minor training injuries and painful rolled ankles have not slowed her down. "I heal quickly," she says with a smile. Bourgeois schedules training runs between a job and caring for her children.

Bourgeois trained diligently so that she would peak on the Fourth of July in 2006. But fate threw a wrench in her plans. Bourgeois ate something that didn't agree with her the night before the race and she began to throw up. After the race she explained to an *Anchorage Daily News* reporter, "There was a point where I thought I would accept defeat, but then I said, no. I'm not going to let it stop me, I've worked too hard." After a restless night, Bourgeois's goal was just to finish the race. But after reaching the base of the mountain she began to feel better and pushed herself on the climb. Downhill is her strength and she bound down in 12:46 to win her third race in 52:33, the eighth fastest women's finish in race history. Bourgeois extended her winning streak and got faster over the next two years. She finished in 52:21 in 2007 and in 52:11 in 2008.

Bourgeois's fans love to relive and retell the events leading up to her photo finish win in 2010. After trailing Holly Brooks at the top of the mountain and down the waterfall, Cedar managed to catch Brooks near the finish line and pull ahead to win by ten seconds in 51:48. Bourgeois's run was the sixth fastest women's finish and her seventh straight Mount Marathon win.

After the race Bourgeois announced her retirement from the race. "I want to spend more time with my kids and I've started a new business. It's time to take a break," she said.

Although Bourgeois sat out the 2011 Mount Marathon Race she did compete and win the Dipsea Quad race, a grueling twenty-eight-mile mountain run in California, in the fall of 2011.

When Bourgeois dipped her feet into the waters of athletic possibilities on her first Mount Marathon Race in 1997, she wasn't chasing fame or wealth; she wanted to test herself, to see if she had the right stuff to become a champion. She did. In the years since that fateful day, Bourgeois has earned accolades from the running community, and garnered the love and respect of Seward fans.

Kikkan Randall

The stars were in alignment on July 4, 2011, when Kikkan Randall won the Mount Marathon Race and racked up the seventh fastest women's finish in 52:03. She was the one who lined them up through talent, enthusiasm, and plain old hard work. After seven second- and third-place finishes, Randall's victory was extra sweet. The quad muscles that propelled Randall to the best ever Olympic and World Cup cross-country skiing results of any American woman came through in her Mount Marathon victory.

Randall's birth on New Year's Eve, the last day of the year, was the only event where she came in last. She burst into the world in motion. By the age of one she was on alpine skis, and she played competitive soccer at the age of five. Her joy in moving her body was evident in her smile and enthusiasm for all sports. "I enjoyed many sports but got serious about running in the sixth grade," she said.

Folks around the world know Randall for her cross-country skiing prowess, not as a mountain runner. But in Alaska she is recognized as a runner and skier. She's run a five-minute mile on a track, is a perennial Women's Run medalist, and has won the Junior Mount Marathon Race three times. Her family has been involved in running the Mount Marathon Race for generations. "Mount Marathon is such an Alaskan event. My whole family goes to Seward on the Fourth of July to watch the race."

In tenth grade, Randall focused on cross-country skiing, and by the age of nineteen she qualified for the 2002 Winter Olympics. Randall, a three-time Olympian, continues to improve. "I go in and race hard in every competition," she said. With focus and hard work, Randall has racked up an impressive skiing resume: first US Olympic women's top ten, four times Olympic top ten, seven times on World Cup podium, and fifteen times National Championships.

"It's a balancing act to train year-round, find sponsors to help with expenses, volunteer at community events, and have a personal life," she said. Randall is married to Canadian skier Jeff Ellis, who understands and supports Randall's Olympic goals. "My main focus is to do well in the World Cup races and to train for the 2014 Olympics," she said. Randall's long-term goal is to be the first American cross-country skier to medal in the Olympics since Bill Koch's silver in 1976.

Randall trains year-round, six days a week, returning to Anchorage in the summer for dry land training. While in Anchorage, Randall gives countless volunteer hours to the Healthy Futures program that sponsors running events for kids. She also gives twenty school presentations a year and talks to Girl Scout groups, where she shares her story and Olympic dreams. And amazingly she still finds time to teach skiing skills to 280 young girls in the Fast and Female program.

Randall's brother Tanner is one of her biggest fans. "She's just so together. It's totally bewildering to me, and inspiring." Randall's Alaskan fans couldn't agree more. In between her Olympic workouts and World Cup races, Randall is hard at work aligning the stars and will no doubt have them in a row again come the next Fourth of July.

Holly Brooks, Seventh Fastest Women's Run

When Holly Brooks crossed the Mount Marathon finish line in 2012 carrying an American flag, she exemplified the American spirit of high aspirations and can-do attitude. "I like the pursuit of excellence," said Brooks, after winning the race in 51:53. "I love setting goals and working hard each and every day to achieve them. There is something extremely satisfying to strive to be the best you can be, whether you win the race or simply finish it," she said. Brooks broke her personal best record by five seconds and added another top ten finish to her resume. "This win meant a lot to me. I'd come up short for a number of years in a row," she said.

Brooks first heard about the Mount Marathon Race in 2008 from skiing friends. "Skiers all know about the Seward Fourth of July race," said

Brooks. "I heard the news that I'd won a coveted lottery spot on my birthday. It was a wonderful present." She finished second in 55:24.

One year later, Brooks's Mount Marathon Race ended in disaster. That year the Fourth of July was an unusually hot day and Brooks became dehydrated and was forced to detour to the hospital. A few hours later she checked herself out of the hospital and walked to the finish line. "I was leading the race at the top, and then three-fourths of the way down the mountain Bourgeois and Randall passed me. I felt light-headed and luckily, a friend who's a nurse literally pulled me off the course before I passed out. My last memory was of her telling me that I couldn't continue the race. The next think I knew, I woke up in the Seward emergency room."

Holly was suffering from exertional rhabdomyolosis, a condition where she basically used up all the moisture in her body. Dehydration plus the motion of running down the mountain ripped her quad muscles, causing extensive damage. "I could hardly bend my legs at my own wedding; I also had a blood blister on my heel the size of an orange that needed to be drained before I could fit into my wedding shoes."

While lying in the emergency room Brooks had an epiphany. "It took this episode, the adrenaline and emotions involved, to make me realize that I wanted to make the 2010 Olympic team," she said.

There was something painfully similar about Brooks's 2010 and 2011 Mount Marathon finishes. In 2010, Brooks was ahead of Bourgeois until a few feet from the finish line and had to settle for second place, and then one year later, in 2010, Randall did the same thing, overtaking Holly a few feet from the finish line.

What a difference a year can make in the life of an athlete. Brooks went from being the last woman across the finish line in 2009, and two second-place finishes in the next two years, to a win in 2012. "I had no idea I was going faster in 2012; in fact, I was certain I was going slower. The conditions were slippery and I had to use my arms to pull myself up the mountain," said Brooks. She prefers to do a sitting glissade in the big trough. "I like the foolproof nature of the big chute. It gives my legs a small break and I don't have to worry about sliding off course or into the rocks. Once on Main Street I was taking my time, enjoying the moment. I didn't see the clock until I was ten seconds from the finish. I had to 'kick it in' to ensure a personal record."

Like many Mount Marathon champions, Holly competes in mountain runs and ski races. "I'm a late bloomer. I skied for five years with the Pacific Northwest Junior Olympic team and skied competitively at Whitman College," said Brooks. After impressive finishes in the US Super Tour, Brooks was

With an American flag held high in triumph, Holly Brooks crossed the finish line during the 2012 race, where she posted the seventh fastest women's finish.

picked for the US 2010 Olympic Cross-Country Ski Team. "Being picked for the 2010 Olympic Team surprised me and the skiing community because I was not a full-time athlete," she said.

After moving to Alaska, Brooks became head coach for the West High School Ski Team. Two years later she began a four-year stint as head junior coach at Alaska Pacific University Nordic Ski Center, and helps coach adult masters and a women's only ski group.

In 2012 Brooks made the 2014 Olympic Cross-Country Ski Team, and her focus for the next two years will be on the Olympics. "Being a professional athlete takes a high level of satisfaction and dedication. There are great days and there are trying days, but I wouldn't trade it for anything. You learn so much about yourself and your limitations. I also love being outside, I love training in the mountains, and I love being fit and healthy," said Brooks.

Since the 2013 Mount Marathon Race is only six months from the Sochi Olympics Games in Russia, Brooks will have to see whether she races or sits out the event in Seward. "I love the race and can hardly stand the thought of sitting it out but I invest a lot in my ski career and Mount Marathon has caused lots of injuries."

Seward fans will abide by Brooks's decision in 2013, knowing that she will return to the race one day with her competitive spirit and smile intact.

Tom Besh: Daughters Continue His Legacy

"He loved mountains and climbed like a mountain goat," is the way family and friends describe Tom Besh, the third man to run a sub-forty-five-minute Mount Marathon Race in 44:59 in 1977. Like many previous winners, Besh had skied at the Olympic level before retiring to coach at the University of Alaska.

Besh had a burning desire to win the race in 1977, and was willing to put in the extra training hours needed to compete with record holder Bill Spencer, who had already run three sub-forty-minute Mount Marathon Races. Besh ran up and down untold mountains, increased his speed interval workouts, and did hundreds of deep knee bends.

On the Fourth of July, binocular-equipped spectators watched Besh and Spencer battle for position, fighting for the lead as they raced up and down the mountain. When they reached the street at the bottom of the cliffs, Besh, who was stronger on the road section, pulled ahead. Spencer, nursing a familiar side ache, finished second. Besh's big smile said it all. He'd just run a personal best in 44:59. It was a double header for the Besh family. His wife, Judy Ziemlak, had won the women's race earlier in the day.

Besh died in an airplane accident in April 1993, at the age of forty-six. His oldest daughter, Kendra Besh, said about her dad, "Everything was an adventure for him. He took me on many 'little hikes' that turned into six- to eight-hour outings. He carried sausage, cheese, and gumdrops, but we couldn't eat until we reached the top of the mountain. I treasured every minute I spent with dad. Like the time he flew us to Seward so that he could show me the Mount Marathon route when I was eight years old. And the time we hiked the Resurrection Trail, to set up a water station for runners. I was afraid he'd get away from me so I held on to his backpack strap. And we always celebrated the Fourth of July in Seward. It was a family tradition. My aunts always sat on chairs at the corner of Fourth and Jefferson to cheer family members as they ran by."

Kendra remembers her dad telling her that after he got his first pair of wooden cross-country skis he fell in love with the sport. He skied to and from school all winter long. Athletic talent and hard work propelled Besh to a spot on the Junior National cross-country team and a scholarship to ski in Durango, Colorado. He returned to Alaska after college to coach the UAA ski team.

Besh's youngest daughter, Leah, was seven years old when her dad died. "Although Dad never took me up Mount Marathon, he did take me on many backcountry adventures. Like the time he took me with him on a sheep counting trip in the mountains near Dillingham." These trips made a lasting impression on Leah. "I feel at home in the mountains and on wilderness trails."

Leah has competed in the Mount Marathon Race since she was nine years old, and won the junior race twice: in 2002 in 35:22 and 2003 in 35:45.

Her mother, Judy Ziemlack, prepared her for her first race. "I wanted to pass on to Leah what her father had taught me. So that when she comes down Mount Marathon she knows that she's covering the same footsteps as her

Tom Besh became the third man to run a sub-forty-five-minute race in 1977.

father." During her four runs as a senior, Leah has improved her time each year and finished fourth in 1:00:52 in 2007.

Tom Besh, who posted the tenth fastest finish ever in the Mount Marathon Race, lives on in his daughters, who delight in retelling the adventures they shared with their dad.

Nina Kemppel: Nine-time Winner with Longest Winning Streak

Four-time USA Olympic Cross-Country skier and eighteen-time US Cross-Country Champion Nina Kemppel is recognized the world over as an Olympic athlete, but in Alaska she's best known as the woman who's won nine Mount Marathon Races. She blazed her way into the record books and the hearts of Seward fans with her wins from 1994–2003.

Attack, attack, attack, is the way Kemppel describes her Mount Marathon strategy. "Running Mount Marathon takes total gutless courage. It's really an addictive thing. You have to be in a zone. It's really neat to battle with yourself," Kemppel told an *Anchorage Daily News* reporter after running a personal best finish in 54:20 in 2000. She holds the record for the longest streak of wins in Mount Marathon history.

She ran the Mount Marathon Race a month after summiting 20,320-foot Mount McKinley with her father, Roger Kemppel, on June 7, 1995. Gasping for breath at the finish line she told an *Anchorage Daily News* reporter, "This was twenty-five times as hard."

If summiting Mount McKinley a month before the run didn't slow Kemppel down on race day, then a pair of borrowed shoes wouldn't be a problem. "She came by my houses the day before the race to borrow a pair of shoes," said Ellyn Brown. "Nina had six pair of running shoes with her, but they didn't have the grip needed for the Mount Marathon terrain. She was able to win the race in my old, ready-to-fall-apart shoes, which is one of the reasons I really admire her. She has strength and mental and physical toughness. Skiing was always her primary focus and she didn't do a lot of mountain training and still won the race consistently for almost a decade."

Folks around Anchorage, Alaska, who followed her athletic career, always knew Kemppel was bound for athletic glory. Although small for her age, Kemppel dreamed of being an Olympic runner and by the age of twelve was running up to eighty miles a week. Her doctor worried about the effects of such long runs on her adolescent body. But a quote on her website puts those fears to rest. "I was really short for my age and my doctor said I might stunt my growth with too much running. Well, at fifteen I grew eight inches in one year and went from being the smallest to the largest girl in my class."

Nine-time winner Nina Kemppel holds the record for the longest winning streak among women.

Kemppel left her dreams of becoming an Olympic runner behind and decided to become an Olympic cross-country skier when she was in high school. She discovered that skiing was more fun than running during Alaska's cold, dark winter months. By the time she graduated with honors from West High School in 1987 she'd earned two Skimeister awards at the state high school Nordic ski championships.

Kemppel explains on her website how she stayed motivated to train three to four hours a day for the next thirteen years. "It's not about the money, it's not about the glory, it's what I love to do."

Nina Kemppel is not the only family member to make a name for herself on Mount Marathon. Her mother, Mary Kemppel, set a sixty to sixty-nine age group record in 2002 in 1:28:50. Her father, Roger Kemppel, is a perennial top five finisher in his age group and Nina's sister Denali was a competitive cross-country skier in college. After securing her ninth win on Mount Marathon in 2003, Kemppel stepped away from the race to enter the Tuck School of Business at Dartmouth College for two years of graduate school.

When Kemppel returned to the race in 2006 her only goal was to beat her father, a top age group finisher. When word spread about the father-daughter duel, Nina commented to an *Anchorage Daily News* reporter, "Now that we've made it public, it's going to be embarrassing when he beats me."

Youth won the day. Nina's finish time was twenty seconds faster than her dad's. Kemppel is now the CEO and president of the nonprofit Alaska Humanities Forum.

Brad Precosky: Downhill Demon

"My first Mount Marathon Race in 1989 humbled me," said Brad Precosky, six-time Mount Marathon champion.

Cocky and tough after years of skiing, hiking, and running in Colorado and Alaska, Precosky had developed a reputation as a hotshot contender in the mountain-running community. After reading an article about the Mount Marathon Race in the *Anchorage Times*, Precosky drove to Seward on the day of the race confident that he'd blow the competition away.

That year the men's race was limited to two hundred entrants. Precosky stood in line until 10 A.M. to buy a bib for twenty dollars when a runner failed to show up.

Precosky had never been up Mount Marathon nor had he seen the course. Not knowing that the first part of the race was run on the street, he went out too fast, wearing the wrong type of shoe. He got lost on the ridge, crawled in and out of a snow tunnel coming down the chute, and still ended up a top forty finisher. He credits other runners' words of encouragement for his inaugural finish time of 1:04:00. "It was one of the hardest things I've ever done," he said. "I really underestimated the difficulty of the race."

As Precosky crossed the finish line, humbled and exhausted, he looked back at Mount Marathon with a burning desire to be the fastest man on the mountain. Precosky combines the spiritual and the physical in his running. Each year he sets running goals for himself and then puts in the training hours to reach them. He strives to do his best in each competition and when training for an event, everything else on his to-do list recedes.

Precosky's strong work ethic and passion for mountain running has earned him six first-place wins in the Mount Marathon Race. His personal best finish time of 45:07 in 2001 is the eleventh fastest run on record. Competing as a world-class athlete has brought Precosky many moments of joy, including an amazing run down from the top to the finish line in 10:15, which Trond Flagstad matched in 2008. "Someone may have had a faster run down in the early years of the race, but no one was keeping track of the descent time," he added.

He's also had his share of lows. In 1995 he sustained a knee injury in a sledding accident on Flattop Mountain bordering Anchorage, Alaska. Three years later he shattered a hip bone on the same mountain in a snowboarding accident. His last injury occurred during the 2006 Mount Marathon Race when he "redlined," or lost control, and fell on the shale, slicing his right knee. Although bloody and bruised, he pulled off a first-place finish before disappearing into the medical tent.

Precosky, with a degree in biology, lives a minimalist life in a cabin near Anchorage and plows snow for a living. He trains year-round with a group of mountain running friends. These friends sponsored a fund-raiser for Precosky to help him pay medical bills after his hip surgery in 1998.

During the winter of 1998–99 Precosky and Barney Griffith planned and initiated a running series for Alaskan runners to promote development of the sport in Alaska. "Mountain running meant everything to me then," Precosky said. "Griffith and I, with the help of Brian Hall, created the Alaska Mountain Cup in 1999, which evolved into Alaska Mountain Runners, a nonprofit organization." Although committee members have changed, Precosky is still the historian and chairman of the group and does all the posting on the website, alaskamountainrunners.org, which documents the Grand Prix results. "I felt it was time to give back to the racing community," he added.

Precosky was a member of the US Mountain Running Team at the 2001 World Mountain Running Trophy in Arta Terme, Italy. He returned home with a burning desire to host a World Running Trophy Race in Alaska. Later that year he presented and won the bid to have a race at Mount Alyeska in 2003 and then spent the next two years working to make it happen. Giving speeches and raising money are not Precosky's favorite activities, but with the help of friends he was able to raise the two hundred thousand dollars necessary to finance the race.

Brad Precosky ran an epic 10:15 downhill run.

When his own funds ran out due to a poor snow year, he was forced to sell off some of his land to keep himself afloat while he worked on this project. During the five months before the race, Precosky worked twelve hours a day lining up sponsors and a small army of volunteers and was unable to compete in the race himself. Despite all this, he was quick to add, "It was the most rewarding experience of my life."

Precosky said that turning forty and joining the "old guys club" has changed his perspective. Finishing first isn't as important as it was in his twenties. But he wants any runner who beats him to work for it. He likes to see a high level of competition and plans to compete as long as he can.

He set a forty to forty-nine age group record with his win in 2007 and he follows in the footsteps of Volker and Boonstra as one of the oldest men to win the race. With his record of fourteen top five finishes, twelve sub-fifty-minute runs, and six first-place wins in the Mount Marathon Race, he's earned the respect of runners and fans alike.

After the birth of his son Braun in November of 2007, Precosky faced a new and very different challenge. After a few months of sleepless nights he said, "I think I'm getting the hang of being a father."

Jeff Johnson: Three-time Consecutive Winner 1978–80

Trail conditions were excellent on race day in 1980, with dry track going up and a large snowfield at the top. Twenty-three-year-old Jeff Johnson attacked the downhill section of the run with daredevil abandonment to win his third consecutive Mount Marathon Race in 46:35. "Praise the Lord, man, I'm done," he told a *Daily News* reporter. "I feel good right now." He had won the previous two races, in 46:17 in 1979 and in 46:46 in 1978.

It's ironic that Johnson's fastest finish in 1976 in 45:32 didn't garner him a win. But when your competition is Bill Spencer, who won in 44:25, it's understandable. Although Johnson didn't get a first-place medal, he did join a small group of elite runners who've run the race in less than forty-six minutes. He's also run five sub-fifty-minute runs and is the twelfth fastest man to run the mountain.

Todd Boonstra: Oldest Man to Win the Race

Todd Boonstra, four-time winner, with three consecutive wins from 1996–98, and the oldest man ever to win the race, is also the ninth fastest man to run Mount Marathon with a personal best of 45:17 in 1997.

When asked which accomplishment he is most proud of, he said, "Since I didn't think I had a chance to win the race in 2003, I guess I'd have to say that being the oldest man to win made me feel pretty good." Boonstra and his wife are teachers at Galena, a small village on the Yukon River, about three hundred miles west of Fairbanks, Alaska. "Galena has thirteen miles of road and I trained by running it, and was only able to climb Mount Marathon one time before the race." The base he established as an Olympian pulled him through. Boonstra cross-country skied on an Olympic team for thirteen years and participated in three Olympics before retiring in 1995. He also skied on five World Championship and five World University teams, and was the only American to medal.

Boonstra watched his first Mount Marathon Race after moving to Alaska in 1995. The mountain looked intimidating, but after cheering wife-to-be Kelli Jo Linderman across the finish line, he said, "If she can do it, I can do it."

Since then he's run the race seven times, winning four. The 2003 race was a family affair, wife Kelli Jo finished sixth in the women's race (she placed second in 1999) and three-year-old daughter Riana won the three-year-old sprint on Fourth Avenue. After the race, Riana told her dad, "I won; now you gotta win."

Boonstra explained his strategy: "Many runners are faster on the downhill section, so I tried to reach the top ahead of the pack, but [Frode] Lillefjell, a NCAA champion, beat me to the top by about twenty seconds. By the time we reached the street, I'd made up a few seconds and was able to pull ahead on the road."

"When I heard that a junior girl had torn her spleen during the race, I went to see her at the hospital to give her my bib, hoping to cheer her up. Much to my surprise and delight, I found out that Brad Precosky, Barney Griffith, and Clint McCool, perennial top five finishers, had the same idea. They'd already been to see her. It says a lot about the mountain running community.

"Right now I have no plans on returning to the race. My priorities changed after the birth of our three daughters. We ski, hike, and snowshoe as a family and I get lots of strength training by splitting all our firewood."

Out of the 905 participants in the 2007 Mount Marathon Race, 90.8 percent were Alaskans, nine percent—or eighty-nine runners—were from out of state, and two racers were from overseas.

Age Group Record Holders 2007–12

Sheryl Loan: Fifty to Fifty-nine
Age Group Record Holder

In her first Mount Marathon Race, a fifty-three-year-old mother of three from Eagle River, Alaska, set a new fifty to fifty-nine age-group record in 2012 by finishing in 59:23. She set a goal, stayed focused, and did the work needed to beat Carmen Dunham's record. "My goal was to finish in under an hour, which would automatically break Dunham's record, set in 2006 in 1:01:28," said Loan after her amazing finish.

Three years earlier Loan and her family had watched the Mount Marathon Race for the first time. The following year, she and her daughter hiked up to the halfway point. As she watched the women race by, she said, "I'm going to be too old to run this race if I don't get into next year's race."

Loan was well aware of the odds of getting her name drawn in the lottery so she wrote a letter to the race committee seeking a special invitation to run the race citing her many state and national cycling records. When she received a confirmation letter in March 2012, along with a bib number, she was thrilled.

During the four months prior to the Mount Marathon Race, Loan set two new age-group records. She'd never been to the summit of Government Peak before race day and still managed to set a record in 1:00:37. Two weeks later, Loan earned a second record in the Bird Ridge Race, with her finish in 52:44.

With two records under her belt, Loan set her sights on Mount Marathon. Since Loan had never been to the summit of Mount Marathon before her first training run in the spring of 2012, her friend Tiffany Novakovich offered to give her some pointers on how to traverse the cliff area. "I've explained this to my kids, so I can show you," Tiffany said.

"Tiffany showed me where to find handholds on the route up through the roots and where to put my feet coming down the cliff," Loan said. "I was worried about the snowfield at the top, because it's so steep and I was concerned that I might not be able to stop at the bottom. But after two practice runs I felt confident about my ability to control my descent," she added.

Reports of a mud slide on the uphill course were also worrisome to Loan, but by the start of the women's race the course had dried. Loan powered up the mountain and was the third racer to reach the summit. Finishing seventh overall, she ran faster than athletes young enough to be her daughter. Loan didn't know that she'd set a new record until after she crossed the finish line.

Loan's competitive career began after joining Mountain Bikers of Alaska in 1986. The club's many competitive and social events fit into Loan's lifestyle. After the birth of her first child in 1988, and wanting to utilize her time efficiently Loan found herself a fitness coach. With both a job and a family Loan needed a workout schedule she could do on her own. After her coach, Zenon Babray, left the state to become head coach for University of Southern California's rowing team, Loan started to receive her workout schedules once a month, via e-mail.

Loan squeezes in workouts between her job as a dental hygienist and being a mom. With a husband and children who also love cycling, the Loan family often celebrates family birthdays with long mountain-bike rides and dinner out.

"Sharing hikes up Mount Baldy, a climb behind our home in Eagle River, is a bonding time for the kids and me. We've seen some awesome sunsets, eagles, and even ran into a little black bear." Her oldest son is in the military, her daughter a freshman at Alaska Pacific University (APU), and youngest son a high school senior. Both younger children are competitive skiers, bikers, and runners. They've put their name in the Mount Marathon lottery hoping to get a chance to run the race with their mom in 2013.

Hardly skipping a beat after her triumph on Mount Marathon, Loan was the first woman to the top of Mount Alyeska in 31:44:8 in August

2012. Then in September she traveled to Bend, Oregon, to compete in the eighty-kilometer Cycling Master's Road National Championships, where she finished third.

The summer of 2012 was a winning season for Loan, who competed in twenty cycling and mountain running events, setting state and national records. She found a formula that works for her: set goals, stay in prime physical condition, and work hard. Loan hopes to improve her downhill time during the 2013 Mount Marathon Race and when Loan sets a goal, watch out. Odds are she'll meet and exceed expectations.

Theresa Brady

Alaskan-born Theresa Brady, a flight attendant now living in White Salmon, Washington, set a new record in the women's forty to forty-nine age group in 2007 in 58:42, seven years after watching her first Mount Marathon Race in 2000. She'd already run two sub-sixty-minute races before her record-breaking run in 2007. At her sister's urging, Brady bought a five-dollar raffle ticket for a chance on a bib in 2006. Though she was a returning runner, she'd missed the 2005 race and lost her eligibility status. Much to her astonishment her name was picked in the raffle and she ran the race the next day without practicing on the mountain. When she finished the race in 2006 in 1:02:06, fifteen seconds under Pam Richter's forty to forty-nine age group record set in 2000 in 1:01:50, Brady said, "'I can pretty easily get the record if I train for the race, and I made that my goal for the next year.'

"The race has turned into a family reunion for our family," Brady said. "My niece Holly Brooks, who finished second; my sister Trish Kopp, who finished eighteenth; and nephew all ran the race in 2008. And my mom and the rest of the family come to Seward to cheer for us and to celebrate the Fourth of July."

It wasn't until Brady ran track and cross-country at Northern Colorado at Greeley that she developed into a competitive runner. "I was always outside playing as a kid and wasn't involved in organized sports," she said. "Then in high school I discovered aerobics and became certified as an instructor and spent many years traveling around the world training other instructors. Exercise is a lifestyle choice for me—I'm an avid cyclist and windsurfer and have just discovered randonee skiing. I climbed Mount Adams [Washington] in mid-June and Mount Hood [Oregon] in mid-July of this year and skied down from the top. I love it," she said.

Alaskan Age Group Record Holders
Thomas Coolidge

Most runners slow down with age, but not sixty-one-year-old Thomas Coolidge. He ran his fastest finish in 1:00:06 on his twentieth run up the mountain in 2011, setting a new record in the sixty to sixty-nine age group. He admits that a few things have changed since his first race in 1989, when he hadn't trained on the mountain. "Every time I reached a summit, I looked up, and there was another one. Now I know they are called false summits," he said. He attributes familiarity with the mountain and an improved training schedule for his faster speed year after year.

In 2011, Coolidge struck gold over and over again, setting new age group records in every event he competed in. To build up his endurance, Thomas trained and skied his sixth Susitna 100, completing the 100-mile ski race in twenty-three hours. Any athlete looking to build endurance should check out this ski race. It's not only long, but most of it takes place in the dark. Competitors must carry at least fifteen pounds of survival gear and a couple liters of water. A few weeks later he ran up Bird Ridge in a blistering fifty-two minutes and in the fall he ran the 26.2-mile Moose's Tooth Marathon. One year earlier, Coolidge ran the Marine Corps Marathon in Washington, D.C., in 3:13:30.

"Attitude is everything. Forget the age and just keep moving," he said. "My ninety-two-year-old mother still gets out and walks every day." Coolidge's love of competition and of staying fit has rubbed off on his two daughters. He and daughter Kelsey trained together for the 2011 Mount Marathon Race. "Her goal is to beat my time," he said. "And she came

Age Group Race Records (as of July 2012)

Men's

18–29	Bill Spencer	00:43:21	1981
30–39	Trond Flagstad	00:44:03	2008
40–49	Trond Flagstad	00:44:26	2012
50–59	Barney Griffith	00:48:23	2006
60–69	Thomas Coolidge	01:02:58	2012
70-79	Fred Moore	01:07:09	2010
80-89	Corky Corthell	01:52:59	2009

Women's

18–29	Nancy Pease	00:50:30	1990
30–39	Carmen Young-Dunham	00:50:54	1986
40–49	Teresa Brady	00:58:42	2007
50–59	Sheryl Loan	00:59:23	2012
60–69	Elaine Nelson	01:19:36	2007
70+	Mary Hensel	01:57:02	2008

close. She was only two minutes slower than me." Then the proud father continued, "Kelsey came in tenth in the women's race."

"I try to train smart," he said. "I work out with the Alaska Winter Stars, a master's ski group which is a focused training program. In the summer, I add interval workouts. Then in the months before the Mount Marathon Race I spend more hours in the mountains."

Barney Griffith

"It's the best snow conditions I ever saw," Barney Griffith said after setting a new record in the fifty to fifty-nine age group in 48:23 in 2008, shaving four minutes off Eddie Baxter's 2005 record run in 52:59. Griffith continued, "I ran to get up speed at the top and slid on my butt on the snow in the steep areas." Only six men crossed the finish line ahead of him.

Griffith's winning run was no accident. He set his goals for a record run as soon as he crossed the Mount Marathon finish line in 2007. He stayed focused and put in extra training hours. Starting in November he climbed Bird Ridge, a 3,500-foot mountain outside of Anchorage, every Sunday at noon regardless of the weather. Between climbs he mountain biked and ran trails. He spent a month on the South Island in New Zealand in midwinter to get away from the snow and do more running. As the Fourth of July grew closer, Griffith's training became more intense. He and his mountain running buddies challenged each other by racing up Flattop Mountain. With training runs on Mount Marathon consistently under 49:00 Griffith was confident he'd set a record, barring an accident.

Barney Griffith's Mount Marathon records started with four wins in the junior race.

This amazing mountain runner did admit to prerace jitters. "I didn't sleep too well for two nights before the race."

Griffith's love of mountains and competitions comes naturally. His father, Dick Griffith, a legendary mountain man, competed in the 200-mile Iditaski race, part of the four-division Iditasport competition, at the age of sixty-five. And in 2007 at the age of eighty he ran the Alaska Mountain Wilderness Classic, a 150- to 250-mile backcountry race that crosses mountain ranges and untracked wilderness.

Griffith was raised in the foothills of the Chugach Mountains and was climbing Flattop alone by the time he was eight years old. In junior high he won the state cross-country skiing championship and competed in the Nordic Junior National Championships.

"I love to be in the beautiful mountains. Competing is part of a healthy lifestyle choice that I share with friends. Sometimes an old back or knee injury flares up, but I feel fortunate to be able to compete at my age," he said.

Griffith's Mount Marathon record is impressive: Four Junior Mount Marathon wins, a personal best finish in 2005 in 46:54, twelve sub-fifty-minute finishes, and a record in the fifty to fifty-nine age group.

Runners are always looking for that extra something that will give them an edge on race day. Griffith tried tweaking his diet. Over the past year he drank green smoothies, ate less meat, and cut out a few beers. It paid off. He broke his 2011 record in the fifty to fifty-nine age group by fourteen seconds.

Elaine Nelson

Elaine Nelson ran a personal best in 1:19:36 in her seventh Mount Marathon Race in 2007, setting a new record in the sixty to sixty-nine age group by chopping two minutes off of Edda Stickle's record set in 2004. After watching her first Mount Marathon Race in 2000, Nelson said, "I saw the people coming off the mountain and thought, if they can do it, so can I."

Nelson, a petite woman, said, "I tell people I'm five-foot-two, but I think I'm really only five-feet-one-and-a-half-inches tall." She needed the height, even if it was imaginary, the four years she played on the first UAA Women's Basketball Team from 1974 to 1978. "They were desperate," she added.

Growing up on a cattle ranch near the Canadian border, Elaine Nelson rode horses instead of bicycles and learned how to can food and cook for her dad and four brothers. Although Nelson and her husband arrived in Anchorage in 1968 she didn't run her first footrace until 1979. And she didn't get serious about her training until 1983 when she joined the YMCA's Women's Running Team and ran her first marathon. "I've been running ever since," she said. "Since then I've run over fifteen marathons and many 5K and 10K races. I found my niche. Running is a social activity for me—I find runners to be good people," she said.

In 1997 she started training for mountain runs with Corky Corthell and later that same year set a record in the fifty to fifty-nine age group in the sixteen-mile Lost Lake Run in 2:38:00. "I have dreams of doing more cross-training when I retire," Nelson said. "But right now I run every day all year long." She's won age group records in many of the Alaska Mountain Running Grand Prix races and has no plans on retiring from competition.

Jerre Wills

After seventy-year-old Jerre Wills, of Homer, Alaska, set a new age group record in 2007 in 1:16:52, he commented, "This race is as rewarding as anything you can do on the planet." Trim and muscular as a man half his age, Wills works hard to keep in competitive shape. He trains year-round, but ups his mountain climbs when training for the Mount Marathon Race. A few weeks before the Fourth of July, Wills drives to Seward and sets up a tent at the base of Mount Marathon. He climbs the mountain twice a day for a week. The rest of the year his schedule includes hundreds of sit-ups a day, weight lifting, leg lunges, track speed work, skipping rope, and snowshoeing. Wills, in what may be the understatement of the year, said, "I've been way too competitive all my life."

Wills's oldest daughter, Cheryl Ess, fifty-three, finished in 1:16:15 in 2008, and is a perennial top five age group winner. His wife, Winnie, stood on the sidelines and cheered for her husband and daughter. She'd been sidelined with knee problems after having run the race for many years.

As a longtime commercial fisherman in Homer, Wills put his heart and soul into his business and didn't get serious about medaling in the race until after he retired. "The race is special to me because of the Seward people," he said. "They're like family welcoming you back every year."

Mary Hensel

Seventy-year-old Mary Hensel is just hitting her stride. She broke the record in the seventy to seventy-nine age group by forty-six minutes with her finish in 1:57:03 in 2008. This was her third win in the 2008 Grand Prix race series, the first seventy-year-old woman to achieve that goal.

Organized sports were not an option for Hensel, who grew up on a farm family in Illinois in the '40s and '50s. The Catholic elementary school she attended didn't offer any extracurricular sports activities. Although the Catholic high school she attended did offer after-school sports activities, she didn't have transportation home and couldn't participate.

It wasn't until after the birth of her six children that Hensel got involved in skiing in 1972 when her daughter Ann joined the Junior Nordic ski program. Hensel listened to what the coaches were telling the kids, and then put their advice into practice as she followed the skiers on their practice sessions.

She started running recreationally in 1983 when daughters Michelle and Jill talked her into running the Alaska Women's Run (now the Alaska Run for Women) and the Gary King Sixty Minute Challenge Race (now the Alaska 10K Classic). Ten years later, in 1993, the same two daughters talked her into running the Mount Marathon Race with them.

She has competed in the Grand Prix series since 2002, winning her age division in 2003, 2004, and 2005. She also won the sixty to sixty-nine age open division in the World Mountain Running Trophy held at Alyeska in 2003. She traveled to Ireland in 2007 and placed second in the sixty to sixty-nine age group in the Dublin half-marathon.

Mary Hensel on her record-setting race for the seventy to seventy-nine age group in 2008.

After eleven Mount Marathon runs, two first-place age group wins, and an age group record, Hensel has no plans on retiring. "I do it because it feels so good when I cross the finish line, and as a way to stay healthy," she said. Hansel's daughter Michelle, a doctor in Seward, had to buy her way back into the race in 2007. The mother-daughter duo competed on the slopes of Mount Marathon once again.

Outstanding Athletes - Junior Race Records

Many outstanding athletes have run the Mount Marathon Race since its beginning and have achieved some amazing personal goals. Kjerstin Lastufka, a perennial top five finisher during the years she competed, ran five sub-sixty-minute runs and still managed to come across the finish line looking fresh and clean. In the men's division many perennial top five finishers have amassed some impressive records. Clint McCool has run eight sub-fifty-minute runs and set a few age group records. Competitive and a threat in any race, Darin Markwardt, Eric

Overall Record

Girls	Allison Ostrander	30:32	2011
Boys	Bill Spencer	24:24	1981

(the junior race did not have age group divisions until 1994)

11 and Under Age Group

Girls	Allison Ostrander	35:35	2008
Boys	Aaron Thrall	30:51	1994

12–14 Age Group

Girls	Allison Ostrander	30:32	2011
Boys	Michael Marshall	28:28	2010

15–17 Age Group

Girls	Becky Forbes	31:26	1976
Boys	Miles Knotek	26:18	2011

Strabel, and Shawn Erchinger have all run six sub-fifty-minute runs. Many of the top athletes train together and challenge each other to be the best they can be.

Junior Division Race Course

* The junior race is for racers ages seven to seventeen
* This race follows the same trail to the finish as the senior race, but only goes halfway up the mountain.
* Junior runners round the marker at the halfway point and return down the mountain to the finish line.

Allison (Allie) Ostrander, Fast, Fabulous, and Fourteen

This running star from Soldotna, Alaska, soared into the record books in 2011 when she won the junior girls race in a record setting 30:32. But she didn't stay around to collect her medal because she had to catch a plane that took her to soccer camp.

Ostrander's Mount Marathon career began in 2008, when she crossed the finish line in 35:35, with a smile on her face and blonde ponytail swishing back and forth, to set an age group record for girls eleven and

Allison Ostrander crosses the finish line in the record time of 30:32.

under. Her finish was less than a minute behind seventeen-year-old winner of the junior girls race, Allison Barnwell, who finished in 34:59.

"I was ahead of Allison at the halfway turn around and coming down the waterfall," Ostrander said, "but then I took the safety trail, like my folks told me to, and she went down the cliffs and pulled ahead of me."

"My family are all runners," she said. "It's how we stay in shape. My dad and older sister Taylor have been trying to get into the race through the lottery, but Mom and I are the only ones who made it in. I really like going up the roots at the beginning of the hill climb. Mom and Dad practiced with me so that I knew where to put my hands and feet." Ostrander plays soccer four days a week from April until August and plays basketball and volleyball during the winter.

In 2009, twelve-year-old Ostrander won the junior girls race in 34:24, an unusual accomplishment considering she was competing with girls eighteen and under. One year later in 2010, Ostrander set a new record in the twelve to fourteen age group and blew the other contenders away with her winning time of 31:15. In fact, she broke Aubrey Smith's junior girls record set in 1997 by almost two minutes. Ostrander could have coasted through the 2011 race, but she ran into the record books again and broke her own record with an amazing 30:32 finish.

After a day of rain the race route in 2012 was slick and muddy. Ostrander was hoping to set a new fifteen to seventeen age group record but when she found herself slipping backward on the course she didn't think it was possible. After getting a helping hand from another racer she moved on. Mud or no mud, Ostrander still finished in 32:50 to capture the fifteen to seventeen age group record. She is the first girl to set records in all junior age categories.

Ostrander has talent, a supportive family, and most important, a competitive spirit. Seward fans can't help but wonder what surprises and accomplishments are ahead for this amazing athlete.

Becky Forbes: Junior Girls 15-17 Age Group Record

While searching the archives for Mount Marathon trivia in 2012, Jim Renkert found a newspaper article documenting Becky Forbes's junior girls race record set in 1976 in 31:26. The record of her amazing achievement was lost for years. It wasn't until 2010, thirty-three years later, that Allison Ostrander beat Becky's overall junior race record by eleven seconds in a time of 31:15.

"Becky and her sisters were very competitive," recalled Becky's mother Diane Herbst. She remembers camping with her daughters at the base of Mount Marathon two days before the Fourth of July. "I cooked while the girls practiced on the mountain."

"In those days we flew down the mountain without regards to injuring body parts," said Sue Forbes, Becky's sister. Sue remembers the day her sister won the girls junior race. The Forbes sisters and friend Betsy Haines had a friendly rivalry, taking turns winning the junior race. "I had won the year before and Becky really wanted to beat me. She went out fast. And I wasn't able to catch her," said Sue Forbes.

Becky Forbes was a seventeen-year-old high school runner and cross-country skier when she set the junior girls record in 1976.

Aubrey Smith, Seward's Own

"When I climb mountains, I find my joy. And when I run Mount Marathon I love the support and enthusiasm showered on me by Seward fans." Her own competitive spirit and the desire to do well for Seward fans propelled her to three consecutive wins in the junior race. A local favorite, Aubrey Smith ran the third fastest junior girls race ever in 1997 with a time of 33:01. "While training for the record I climbed the mountain every other day until I knew every single step and handhold."

Smith followed the path of many Mount Marathon champions and skied her way to the Olympics. Although skiing and running were her sports at Seward High School, it was at Northern Michigan University where she developed into

Aubrey Smith's time of 33:01 was the fastest in the junior race since 1997.

an Olympic cross-country skier, competing in the Olympic Winter Games in Turin, Italy, in 2006.

After college graduation and retirement from competitive skiing, Smith took a job as the assistant coach for the women's cross-country team at Williams College in Massachusetts. "I love my coaching job," she said. "The school is highly academic and the students are great."

While involved in competitive skiing, Smith didn't run the Mount Marathon Race and lost her eligibility so she had to buy her way into the race in 2007 for four hundred dollars. She finished a respectable fifth in 59:42. "I didn't feel any pressure; I ran the race to enjoy the camaraderie between the women and the crowd cheering us in." In 2008, she finished faster in 58:57, moving up to a fourth-place finish.

For Love of the Race

Mountain Running Families

In some families the love of mountains and zest for life pass from generation to generation like freckles and curly hair.

Haines Dynasty: The Haines-Randall Family
Lew Haines, Betsy and Debbie Haines, Kikkan Randall

The Mount Marathon Race has been a Fourth of July activity for three generations of Dr. Lewis Haines's family for more than forty years. Haines, a World War II Army Air Corps veteran, ran his first Mount Marathon Race in the '60s. "I won a few age group medals, but I didn't go fast enough to win or have an accident." Although he never led the pack across the finish line in the Mount Marathon Race, he was the first man to run a raft through Hells Canyon on the Snake River in Idaho. After moving his growing family to Washington State in the 1950s he skied Mount Baker and Mount Hood and summited Mount Rainier three times. His running career didn't start until after he moved his family to Alaska in 1964. "I got tired of standing around waiting for my kids to finish their sports activities and decided to run with them. I became a gentleman runner," Haines said. He led by example, playing tennis, skiing, running, and swimming with his kids. Age never dimmed his love of high places. At the age of eighty he climbed Mount Washington. But Haines acknowledged that he still feels the sting of defeat from having to catch a ride in a raft after attempting to backpack over the Chilkoot Trail in southeast Alaska when he was eighty-five years old.

"I realize that life changes as we get older, but emotionally I can't accept the limitations."

Betsy Haines won three consecutive women's races from 1978 to 1980.

Although one of Haines's sons, Chris, ran four sub-fifty-minute Mount Marathon Races, with a personal best finish of 47:37 in 1975, it was one of his daughters, Debbie Haines, who grabbed the first win in 1975 in 1:03:53. At our interview in 2007, Debbie said, "Most people don't know I won a Mount Marathon Race. I'm known around Anchorage as Kikkan Randall's mom. But every now and then, to keep Kikkan humble, I like to remind her that I've won a Senior Mount Marathon Race and she hasn't."

Betsy Haines was the second Haines daughter to win a Mount Marathon Race in 1978 with her finish in 57:38. "I love the whole Mount Marathon experience," she said, "but my favorite memory took place during one of my junior races. I beat my boyfriend to the turn-around point before he caught up with me. The next thing I know he's flying horizontally by, hits his head and rolls, only to jump up and beat me." Her three consecutive wins on Mount Marathon between 1978 and 1980 earned her a perpetual trophy.

Kikkan Randall

One of Haines's granddaughters, Kikkan Randall, ran her first Mount Marathon Race in 1993 at the age of ten. "I absolutely loved my first race in front of such a big crowd," she said. She won the girls junior race three consecutive years, 1998–2000, and set a record for girls twelve and under.

Kikkan Randall's mother said that two of the first words Kikkan spoke as a toddler were "Olympic" and "champion." Her words would prove to be prophetic. Randall placed ninth in cross-country skiing at the

2006 Winter Olympics in Italy, the best finish ever for an American woman cross-country skier.

Randall credits her family for helping her reach her goal to be an Olympic athlete. "I always loved moving my body and enjoyed many different sports. My dad had me on alpine skis when I was one. I played competitive soccer at five, cross-country skied at six, and ran with my dad at seven. Mom and Aunt Betsy coached my junior national cross-country team and Granddad would take me to practice. Both my parents nurtured my athletic goals." By sixth grade Randall was running seriously. At the end of tenth grade she met a coach who encouraged her to focus on cross-country skiing and one year later she was one of the top skiers in her age group at Nordic junior national cross-country ski competitions. "When I was nineteen I qualified for the 2002 Winter Olympics in Salt Lake City and my whole family turned out to cheer me on." Randall went on to win three US national cross-country ski championships.

Kikkan Randall ran her first Mount Marathon in 1993 at the age of ten and set a record for girls twelve and under.

Dressed in red, white, and blue, Randall was easy to spot when she ran her first senior division race in 2001. "I love the pure challenge of the run, the adrenalin rush as I pop off the cliffs near the base of the mountain." Although she won the senior race in 2011, ski training is her primary focus and she doesn't train for the Mount Marathon Race. Her ski coaches discourage her from participating in the race because of the possibility of injury. Randall is happy to show up on race day and enjoy the run, without the pressure of being number one.

Randall achieved another of her goals in 2007 when she became the first American woman to win a World Cup Cross-Country ski race. As his granddaughter's athletic career soars, Haines's is winding down. In a somber mood, he said, "After being diagnosed with Guillain-Barré syndrome in 2006, I lost my sense of balance and had to buy a recumbent bike. But it's too slow—I want to go faster."

Randall won't be competing in the Mount Marathon Race until after the 2014 Winter Olympics. She won her second straight World Cup sprint title in March 2013, and is considered the greatest female cross-country skier in US history. Randall's brother Tanner is one of her biggest fans. "She's just so together. It's totally bewildering to me, and inspiring." Alaskan fans couldn't agree more. In between her Olympic workouts and World Cup races, Randall is hard at work aligning the stars and will no doubt have them in a row again in time for the Olympics in 2014.

Marten and Bahne Martensen

"From the time I was three years old, I wanted to run behind the police car that meets the leader when he comes off the mountain and leads him down Jefferson Street," Marten Martensen said, "but I had to wait until 1990, when I won my first Mount Marathon Race for that to happen. Seward was our family destination on the Fourth of July ever since I was one year old. My dad loved the history of the race and the Seward people. One of my favorite childhood memories was running down Fourth Avenue with my dad, Bahne Martensen, as he sprinted towards the finish line."

When I asked Marten about his athletic role models he answered, "My dad was my hero and best friend." At five feet eight inches, Bahne Martensen was not a tall man but he lived big, pulling family and friends along on the roller-coaster ride of their lives. After finishing work he'd climb Flattop Mountain, return home, have a beer, and dance until everyone tired and went home. This nonathletic farm boy finished ninth grade in Germany, went to mechanics school, immigrated to America, found his way to Alaska, and built the largest car dealership in the state. Bahne hiked

With words of encouragement from his father (left) ringing in his ears, Marten (right) won the senior races in 1990, 1992, and 1995.

and hunted in the mountains, but he never trained as an athlete. On a whim in 1969, Bahne decided to enter the Mount Marathon Race, although he'd never been up the mountain. He fell in love with the event and ran it every year until being diagnosed with cancer in 2002. "He was an absolute madman on the downhill course," said Martin. "He loved snow and pointed his feet down and glissaded to the shale." Which might explain how he ended up in the hospital in 1976. "Since he hadn't practiced on the mountain, he didn't know that a piece of snow had fallen at the end of the snowfield, opening up a crevasse. He flew down the snow and fell into a pit, landing on his seat and hands, joining a few other runners wallowing in the hole. He bounded out and started down the shale before he felt a searing pain in his seat. He reached back and pulled a four-by-six-inch piece of shale out of his buttocks. 'You're bleeding bad,' two women spectators called out. One of them pulled off her windbreaker and wrapped it around Dad's seat and thigh, and then they helped him down the mountain. Meanwhile, Mom and the rest of us were waiting for Dad at the finish line. When he didn't appear we walked up the road to look for him. An ambulance was just bringing him to the hospital when we arrived. Doctors worked on him for six hours, and although I was only six years old, the doctor let me cut the thread on the stitches. Dad was more indignant about having to lay on his stomach in the back of our VW Bus for the ride home than he was about the injury.

"Dad practiced with me on the mountain when I was eleven years old in 1980, to prepare me for my first junior race. Two years later my sister Kersten won the girl's junior race after Dad showed her the trail. The next year Dad whispered in my ear, 'Don't let your sister beat you.' It worked. I crossed the finish line ahead of Kersten. In 1986 when I was seventeen years old Dad said, 'You can win this race.' I thought that might be fun and trained seriously by running up and down Flattop Mountain."

With his father's words of encouragement ringing in his ears, Martensen won the boy's junior race in 1986 in 30:32.

Four years later, in 1990, his dream of following the police car down Jefferson Street came true when he won his first senior race in 47:57. He won again in 1992 and 1995, where he ran a personal best finish in 46:49.

"In the early '90s the whole family, except Mom, ran the race on the Fourth of July. My dad got credit for us kids' athletic achievements, but my mom was just as important. She's a real health nut and cooked whatever nutritious, low-fat, low-sugar foods I asked for. I'm six feet tall and I had to work to keep my weight around 155 pounds for competitions. And Mom was always at the finish line with sweets and a treat."

Both Martensen's parents encouraged his passion for hockey, but sports never came before family. When Marten wanted to stay home to play in a hockey tournament instead of going to Hawaii with his folks, his dad put his foot down: "You're going to Hawaii with the family." Martensen went to Hawaii.

Martensen earned a college degree, became a mortgage broker, and married a woman who ran the Mount Marathon when they were dating. She continued to run the race every year after they married except when she was pregnant with their three sons. After his father's death in 2003, Marten stepped into his father's shoes as owner of Continental Motor Co. Inc. in Anchorage.

After being diagnosed with sarcoidosis (an immune system disorder most commonly affecting the lungs) in 2006, Martensen dropped out of competitive running and now exercises to stay fit. He hunts with his sons, and the whole family hikes, bikes, and skis. "When I'm out in the mountains with my sons I reflect on the serenity my dad felt in the mountains."

When asked if he wants his sons to run the race, Martensen replied, "I'll let them decide. If they do, I'll train with them just like my dad did with me."

Martensen's son Jack, age ten, decided that he'd like to run the junior race in 2008, and Martensen, true to his word, showed him the trail. A Martensen father-son duo was on the mountain again. Four years later the entire Martensen family ran the race.

Foldager Family from Seward, Alaska

"I'm back!" Flip Foldager shouts to the mountain on his first spring climb up Mount Marathon. He and wife, Patti, have been up the mountain hundreds of times on training runs over the past twenty-five years. Their enthusiasm for the race and each other is legendary. They like to race each other to the top of the mountain. "If Flip pulls ahead I grab his heel to slow him down," said Patti, with the hint of a smile.

Patti won the women's run in 1985 and 1993, and ran the thirteenth fastest women's finish, with a personal best in 53:22 in 1991. She's also finished eight races in under an hour, and remains a perennial top five finisher in her age group division.

"I love the snowfield at the top of Mount Marathon and attack it with the tenacity of a Tasmanian devil. Even after all these years the race is still fun," Patti said in 2007. When asked if she'd ever been injured on the mountain, she replied, "In 1990 as I was going up the trail I saw a mother bear with two squealing cubs. The mother bear was trying to protect her cubs and ran straight at me. As I tried to get away I rolled and sprained an ankle."

Patti (left) and Flip (right) Foldager, Seward running legends, have run the race for twenty-five years and are perennial top five finishers in their age groups.

Flip Foldager has run twenty-five Mount Marathon Races, four in less than fifty minutes, with a personal best of 49:27 in 1986. A perennial top five age group finisher, Foldager weighs less now than he did in high school, where he was a cross-country runner and wrestler.

With a little encouragement Flip will explain how he got his name. "My dad, a Bush pilot and hunting guide, was away on a hunting trip when my mom called him to tell him about my birth. After hearing the news he told her 'Better name him Flip, 'cause I just flipped the plane trying to land near Mount Redoubt.'"

Foldager, a City of Seward dock employee, shattered twelve vertebrate in 1999 when he got crushed between the dock and a boat. "Add that to the abuse I gave my back packing meat out of the woods for my dad, and I wasn't sure I'd run the mountain again. If I was a horse the doctor would have shot me a long time ago," Foldager told a Seward *Phoenix Log* reporter later that year.

With fortitude and determination he returned to the race in 2000. He's also run two fifty-mile Resurrection Trail races, and finished twenty-third out of 201 in the sixteen-mile Lost Lake Run in 2007 in 2:05:00.

In a pensive mood, Foldager commented about his injury: "The accident made me appreciate life and savor each day. Standing on a mountaintop or high meadow renews me. I'm happy just to be able to run with my wife on the trails around Seward and the Kenai Peninsula."

Trent Foldager, Flip and Patti's son, remembers his mom taking him and his sisters on training runs up the junior course to prepare them for the race. "It was always safety first with Mom. She didn't allow any foolishness or grandstanding antics," said Trent, whose Mount Marathon career came to a sudden end after his sister Denali breezed by him during a junior race. Then he added, "I haven't set any records on the mountain, but I was born in the same hospital and had the same baby nurse as my dad, and my sisters can't claim that." Trent idolizes his grandfather and wants to follow in his footsteps and become a big game guide. And one day he'd like to write a book about his grandfather's adventures.

The Foldager's twin daughters, Denali and Rubye, ran their first junior race at eight and have run every junior race since they were eleven years old. Denali set a record for girls eleven and under in 2001 in 39:40, and has won the girl's junior race three times. "I like to win," she said, with the confidence of someone who's had her share of success. In 2007, Denali told me that she thought it would be cool to come across the finish line bloody. "The crowds along the street seem to expect it. Blood on a runner's body is a red badge of courage. After nicking my wrist on a rock in the chute, I thought I had it made. But the blood flow was so small no one could see it."

The twins just completed four years of running on the cross-country and track team at Seward High School where their mom is a coach and their dad helped out with practice. Rubye won two state cross-country titles in 2004 and 2006, and in 2007, Denali won a state title in the 300-meter hurdles.

The sisters signed with NCAA Division II California State University, Stanislaus to run cross-country track in 2008. They're excited about being the first in their family to go to college.

The twins turned eighteen in 2008, and moved up to the senior division of the Mount Marathon Race to compete against their mom. A mere twelve minutes separated the Foldager family's finish times. Denali finished fifth overall in the women's senior division in a time of 1:01:00, the second youngest women to finish in the top five. Rubye finished twenty-ninth in 1:11:00, and mom, Patti, finished thirty-eighth in a time of 1:13:04. In the men's division, dad, Flip, posted a finish time of 1:11:24. It was a very good day for the Foldager family.

Flip and Patti have been Mount Marathon volunteers for years. Two months before the race, Patti takes junior runners up the mountain every Sunday at noon. She's unyielding about safety. "If little Joey isn't ready for the race, I tell the parents to wait another year and try again," she said.

Flip has been on the race committee for more than fifteen years, helping set up and take down race-day safety cones and fences, and positioning himself at the bottom of the cliffs during the junior and women's races.

If you should happen to be near the base of Mount Marathon in the spring and hear "I'm back!" echoing down the mountain, you'll know Flip's making his yearly inaugural run.

Kopsack Family from Palmer, Alaska

At an age when most men grow cautious, fifty-three-year-old Braun Kopsack posted the fifth-ever fastest downhill time in the Mount Marathon Race in 11:18 in 2007. A few years earlier he turned an accident into a personal best downhill run. "My feet went out from under me and I somersaulted down the shale. When I popped up onto my feet, blood was spraying from my hand. A piece of shale was sticking clear through my palm. I still made it down in under ten minutes." A perennial top ten finisher, he's run the mountain since he was nineteen years old, and in 2008 finished his thirty-first consecutive run in under an hour. "Active and competitive," is the way Braun Kopsack described himself. "I was the oldest, and Dad started taking me moose hunting when I was five years old. It was difficult trying to keep up with Dad, but he always made me walk on my own two feet."

Although Braun ran track in high school, freestyle wrestling was his favorite sport. He placed third in the Olympic Western Division Wrestling Freestyle trials title and was headed for the finals competition when President Carter decided to boycott the Olympics by pulling our athletes out of competition. Braun's Olympic career was over. Braun says he trains constantly: "It's part of who I am. I want to be fit and healthy." The Mount Marathon Race holds a special place in his heart: "I used to watch Dad run the mountain and wanted to follow in his footsteps."

Braun's son, Legend, born on September 17, 2008, needs a few years to grow before he can follow in his dad's footsteps.

Dick Kopsack, patriarch of the family, won the Mount Marathon Race in 1960 in 55:16. Sven Johansson introduced the elder Kopsack to the race and became his training partner. With a passion for adventure, the Kopsack patriarch homesteaded, hunted, ran dogs, snowmachined, and

For Dick Kopsack (left) and sons Braun (right) and Lance (center), Mount Marathon has been about challenging themselves, being in the mountains, and staying fit.

was said to climb like a goat. "Dad won his age group division in the Crow Pass Crossing and Matanuska Peak races. He kept running even after he was diagnosed with cancer," Braun said. Dick Kopsack ran four Mount Marathon Races with his sons before he died at sixty-seven, in 1997.

Lance Kopsack, ten years younger than Braun, finished second in the 1995 run and is a perennial top ten finisher. He's run four sub-fifty-minute races with a personal best finish in 1997 in 49:35. "I'm not as driven as I used to be; I enjoy being out in the mountains, spending time with God," Lance said. His resume reads a lot like his brother's. He wrestled in high school and ran to keep in shape. He's run every Mount Marathon Race since 1984, and like Braun, his strength is downhill. Lance timed a personal best downhill run in 10:28. The brothers train together on Lazy Mountain near Palmer and have had many close races. Both have run the twenty-six-mile Crow Pass Crossing Race twenty-four times.

In 2011 all but one of the Kopsack family ran the Mount Marathon Race. His wife, Judi, finished in 1:11:20; his son Lyon came in second in the junior boy's race in 27:38; and daughters Alyson and Jacalyn ran the junior girl's race. Alyson finished sixth in 37:47, and daughter Jacalyn finished nineteenth in 43:47. Ten-year-old Brooklyn Kopsack won a spot in the 2012 lottery and ran in her first junior race in 2012. The Kopsack family tradition of celebrating the Fourth of July in Seward has five more torch bearers.

Inspirational Runners
Joe Mortiboy

"I stood at the base and looked toward the summit of Mount Marathon in 2003 and wondered what the old man of the mountain had in store for me. Would he give me a good time or be tough on me?" said Joe Mortiboy. "I had stood at the same spot eighteen years ago as I prepared to run my first race to fulfill an agreement with my PE teacher." His coach at Seward High School recognized Mortiboy's potential as a runner and challenged him to do the race in exchange for an A in his class. He finished the race in less than an hour, in 59:57, and walked away from his PE class with an A.

For the next eighteen years Mortiboy struggled with an alcohol addiction, was hurt by it, and finally left it behind. "Ever since I got sober on February 8, 1996, I tried to get back into the Mount Marathon Race," he said. "I entered my name in the lottery every year, but it was never drawn, so I figured I'd better save money and buy my way in. I walked into the auction on July 3, 2003, with three thousand dollars clutched in my hand, praying it would be enough to get me a bib." It was, and he had money to spare. "Although the eight hundred dollars I spent for my bib was the highest bid for the night, it was the best investment I ever made.

"Before I quit drinking, I drank to extreme. Now I'm compulsive about my training. I run five miles three times a week before work,

Joe Mortiboy described buying into the 2003 race as "the best investment I ever made."

cross-country ski with a headlamp during dark winter days, and climb 3,500-foot Bird Ridge year-round, every Sunday at noon. Exercise is health insurance for me, a way to be physically fit." Nearly six feet tall, Mortiboy tries to keep his weight around 145 pounds by eating lots of fruits and vegetables.

He ran all seven Grand Prix Mountain Races in 2005, and earned the Alaska Mountain Runner's Most Inspirational Award for his commitment to a healthy lifestyle and his volunteer work on trail maintenance. Mortiboy, who works with tile and terrazzo by day, uses the same materials to create trophies in his basement workshop in winter, which he donates to the Alaska Mountain Runners for their Awards Banquet.

One of Mortiboy's Seward High classmates who ran the Mount Marathon Race with him in 1978, Rolf Barthanson, bought into the run in 2007 for a whooping $1,175, and the two trained together again. "Rolf and I race to the top, we're both very competitive. The old man of the mountain hasn't let me break an hour since I was eighteen, although I came close with my finish in 2004 in 1:04:00. I just hope he'll have mercy and give me one more sub-hour run."

Ellyn Brown

Many compare Ellyn Brown's Mount Marathon career to a ball careening down a steep slope: both pick up speed the farther they go. After twenty-five Mount Marathon runs, at age fifty-four, Brown ran a personal best in 2006 in a time of 1:02:15, to capture ninth place overall. Except for the year she rolled her foot over a rock and broke her fibula on a downhill training run three days before the Fourth of July, she's always been a top twenty finisher. In 2004 she set a new age group record for fifty to fifty-nine-year-old women in 1:04:23.

She was raised in Hawaii in a nonathletic, academic family. Brown recalls, "When I was in fourth and eighth grades, our family spent a year in Australia

Ellyn Brown, age fifty-four, ran a personal best in 2006 in 1:02:15, after running the race twenty-five years.

and Papua New Guinea. I was a tomboy and loved to go with my dad, a professor of entomology, as he collected insects."

Before she set off for college, a one-hundred-pound bundle of energy, her father gave her his blessings and a philosophy to live by. "Never falter in climbing great mountains of the spirit or mind."

With her father's words to guide her, Brown set off on her life journey. "After college I came to Alaska in 1976, to work as an exploration field geologist in Fairbanks. I built strength and stamina by carrying rocks up and down steep mountain slopes. But even more important, I developed a love and awe for mountains," she said.

Limitless energy, enthusiasm for life, and a demanding work ethic propelled Brown to become a world-class athlete over the next twenty-five years. It began in Fairbanks, Alaska, in 1980 when she ran her first 10K race. She enjoyed the experience so much that she started running daily for the pure joy of moving her body. That was also the year a friend told her about a crazy mountain run in Seward held on the Fourth of July.

"Two years later I rode the train to Seward," she said, "and signed up to run the race even though I'd never been up the mountain. Only twenty women competed that year and we ran with the men. I followed three men up the gully and along the ridge. Coming down over shale and slippery waterfall was a blast. The cheers from the crowd as I crossed the finish line made me feel like a million bucks. No other crowd comes close to the support and encouragement the Seward crowd showers on all runners."

Nancy Pease, Carmen Young, Nina Kemppel, and Bill Spencer are some of Brown's heroes. "They're beauty in motion, relaxed, humble runners," she said. "During our joint training runs they encourage me by offering strategies and running tips." The camaraderie is one of the reasons she keeps returning to the run.

Before and after the women's race, Brown cheers for participants in the junior and men's races. She reads the race program to match the names with the numbers so she can call out their names as they run by.

Brown switched from road races to mountain trails in the 1990s after her knees rebelled from too many runs on cement. She learned to swim and added strength training and biking to round out her cross-training schedule. Marriage and motherhood didn't slow her down. After son Keeter's birth in February, 1984, Brown wasn't able to train for her Fourth of July run but still finished in a time of 1:30:00.

Switching careers from geology to teaching in 1992, Brown shared her love and enthusiasm for fitness with her students by creating a video presentation in 2002 on her Hawaiian Ironman competition. She told her students how much fun she had celebrating her fiftieth birthday with a 2.4-mile ocean swim, 112-mile bike ride, and 26.2-mile run. "It was a life-changing experience," she said. "It gave me such confidence that I looked around for a new experience."

She won the US Federation Western State Orienteering Championship in 1998 and then went on to win the US Orienteering Federation National Championships in 2003 and 2005.

An amazingly versatile athlete, Brown also won the US Master's Open Snowshoe Championships in 2003. That same year, she journeyed to Antarctica and ran a marathon. "It was a piece of cake," she said, making the twenty-six-mile run sound easy. When one of Brown's former students competed against her in the Gold Nugget Triathlon, the girl turned to Brown and said, "If I can make it through your class, I can do this." Brown responded with a thumbs up. Brown shares her photography talent with the running community by making yearly videos documenting each of the races in the Mountain Running Grand Prix; she served on the Mountain Running Series board of directors for many years. She's won age group records in all the mountain runs, from the twenty-six-mile Cross Pass Crossing to the fourteen-mile, 9,000-foot-elevation-gain Matanuska Peak Challenge. She won the Matanuska Peak women's race in 1997 and was the overall winner in 2003.

Retirement is not in Brown's future. The scrapbook she used to chronicle twenty-five years of runs, climbs, and orienteering achievements was filled to the brim by 2006, and she went out and bought another to hold the next twenty-five years of athletic challenges.

Fred Moore

When Fred Moore completed his forty-second consecutive Mount Marathon run in 2011, he'd run in half of the eighty-four Mount Marathon Races. In 2010, Fred set a new age group record for men seventy to seventy-nine with his amazing run in 1:07:09. He's run twenty-seven of the races in under an hour, with a personal best of 53:25, and he set a record in the sixty to sixty-nine age group in 2000 in 1:00:56. "When I do something, I want to do the best I can," he said. No one exemplifies the Alaskan spirit of rugged individualism, love for the mountain, and community participation better than Moore.

He arrived in Seward in 1959 and liked what he saw. He spent his first few years in Seward commercial fishing. "It was legal to hunt sea lions in those days, and I sold the meat and skins. Now I work as a carpenter when I want, where I want," he said. He and his family live on the outskirts of Seward in a house he built, surrounded by signs of a subsistence lifestyle, a lush garden, chickens and turkeys, and moose antlers above the door.

Moore, trim and muscular as a forty-year-old, keeps active year-round: he climbs, runs, hunts, skis, and snowmachines.

When asked about the sixty to sixty-nine age group record he set in 2000, he commented, "Not all races end so successfully. Some are harder than others. Two days before the Fourth of July race in 2005, my back went out and I had to settle for fifth in my age group. It took pills, brandy, and guts to get me to the finish line."

Moore speaks of his children with love and pride. "My youngest daughter, nineteen-year-old Erin, is a good artist, and my daughter Bonnie graduated from college and is learning Japanese. And my son, Walter, is in the carpentry school in Anchorage. They've run the race since they were kids." Moore's wife, Phyllis, quit the race two years ago when her knees

★ Sandy Johnson, the Price of a Dream ★

Mount Marathon hopeful Sandy Johnson sat in the bleachers of the Seward High School gym clutching her checkbook. The then fifty-eight-year-old Anchorage resident had come to the Marathon bib auction the night before the July 4, 2002, race to buy her way in.

The gym was packed with an overflow crowd seated on the floor around the perimeter of the room. Johnson's eyes darted around the gym. "I wonder how many women are here to buy a bib?" she asked her husband seated next to her.

Sandy Johnson nears the summit.

The crowd roared with excitement as the auctioneer raised his gavel. "Who'll start the bidding at fifty dollars?" Many hands flew into the air. "Who'll give me a hundred?" "Two hundred?" "Three hundred?" Each time the price went up a few hands went down.

Some folks come to Seward just to see the auction. They swear it's more exciting than watching the race.

When the first Mount Marathon Race was run in the early 1900s, no one could have predicted people would one day pay hundreds of dollars for a chance to run up the mountain. Back then, few runners even wanted to take part in the grueling Fourth of July challenge. That changed when runners, nursing their wounds and drinking beer at a local watering hole, declared it was a "blast." Once the rumor started, it was impossible to stop.

At the first auction in 1995, buying a bib was not a problem. Even cash-poor high school runners could participate. But each year the price for a bib went up. Johnson's monetary resources consisted of a second job and a supportive husband. For years she stood on the sidelines, cheering for her husband, Norm. In 2002 she wanted in. The couple agreed that four hundred dollars was the most Johnson could pay for a bib number.

But as all eyes fixed upon the auctioneer that night before the race, the price kept notching upward. "Who'll give me $450?" yelled auctioneer Steve Lemme.

Johnson put her hand down. She grimaced when the bib number went for $450. The scene was repeated eight more times. One bib left.

"Let's start the bidding at five hundred dollars" yelled Lemme. "I've got to get this one," uttered a desperate Johnson.

A young woman with a sleek, trim runner's body, sitting in the bleachers across from Johnson, raised her hand.

"Who'll give me six hundred?"

"Me," yelled Johnson as she jumped up and glared at her adversary across the gym. The crowd cheered.

The auctioneer looked at the young woman. "Will you give me seven hundred?" The girl looked at the woman beside her, a relative no doubt, same face but older. The women nodded. The girl raised her hand. The crowd was on its feet cheering, first for one bidder, then the other. When the young woman hesitated at nine hundred, the auctioneer lowered the bid. "How about $820?" The girl's hand went up. "$840?" A madness gripped Johnson, her eyes glazed over. "Yes," she shouted.

"More, more," the crowd roared.

"$860," cried the young woman as she threw her fist into the air.

Johnson gasped and clutched her chest.

"You can't let it go for twenty dollars," roared the crowd.

The Anchorage television camera zoomed in on Johnson's face. Defiant she yelled, "$880." All eyes focused on the other bidder. The girl looked at the woman beside her. The woman shook her head. It was over.

As a dazed Johnson made her way down from the bleachers to the front of the gym, supporters pushed money into her hands. By the time she worked her way to the front of the building she had two hundred dollars to help pay for her bib number.

Johnson made the television evening news. Strangers stopped her on the street: "Aren't you the woman who paid $880 for a bib number?" No one had ever paid that much for a women's bib number in the history of the auction.

The Fourth of July crowd gave Johnson a round of applause as she attached the bib number to her running shorts. The smile that lit up her face as she lined up for the start of the women's race was still evident beneath the dust and sweat as Johnson stumbled across the finish line. She'd earned her finisher T-shirt.

When people asked if the T-shirt was worth $880, Johnson clutched it tight and replied, "You can't put a price on a dream come true."

gave out, but she'd already received her plaque for completing twenty Mount Marathon runs.

Moore was a Boy Scout leader and has spent untold hours as a Mount Marathon volunteer. He spent many years on the race committee, scouted and helped build the new safety trail, cleans trails, and still works the women's and junior races.

Moore has completed the most consecutive races, forty-three from 1970 to 2012, and at age seventy-two still finishes in the top half of competitors. When asked whether his strength was going up or down the mountain, he replied, "Downhill. I used to get down from the top to the finish line in eleven and a half minutes." Familiarity with the mountain also helps. In reply to the question of how he stays motivated to train and run the mountain year after year, he said, "I never climb a mountain just to get to the top. It's important for me to be alone in the wilderness. I plan on running, climbing, and hiking till I keel over. I won't voluntarily quit the Mount Marathon Race."

Evan Steinhauser

Lady luck smiled on Evan Steinhauser in 2003, when he won a highly prized lottery opening in the Mount Marathon Race in Seward, Alaska, which is limited to 300 men. Anyone who finishes in under two and a half hours can return the next year. And most do. Wannabe runners must put their name into the lottery, or bid for a bib at the auction. With bibs going for thousands of dollars, the only hope for most men is for their name to be picked in the lottery. Which explains why Steinhauser was so ecstatic. He took the lottery win as a sign from the Mountain Gods that he was to run the Mount Marathon Race for ten consecutive years.

Then, still giddy at his good fortune, Steinhauser decided to up the ante. "If I'm going to run Mount Marathon for ten years, why not complete all the Alaska Grand Prix races for ten years?" When reality set in, he added, "It sounded crazy, even to me."

The Alaska Grand Prix consists of six mountain runs from May to

August. The cumulative elevation gain is around 22,000 feet, or the equivalent of climbing Mount Denali, Alaska's highest peak. Some mountain runners will run the Grand Prix now and then, but no one has chosen to run the gamut year after year.

Running the entire series was an ambitious goal for a forty-nine-year-old transplanted Flordian, who had only run recreationally until he arrived in Alaska in 1990. But Alaska, with more mountains than people, casts spells on newcomers who venture onto alpine slopes, and Steinhauser was no exception.

"I learned about the Mountain Running Grand Prix when I photographed many of the races as a staff photographer for the *Anchorage Daily News*. I figured if I could carry heavy cameras 3,400 feet up Bird Ridge, I could finish the race," said Steinhauser.

You won't find Steinhauser's name in the top finishers of any of the mountain races, but that's just fine with him. "I've slowed considerably, but I always have fun, and I always enjoy just being in the same races as some of the incredible athletes we have in Alaska."

Steinhauser's an inspiration for runners who love to run or hike mountains trails for fun, renewal, or as a commitment to a healthy lifestyle. He usually trains alone, running or skiing in the mountains near his home in South Anchorage. "I'm never too sad about summer ending. The skiing in this town is as much fun as running. We are so spoiled to live in such a beautiful place with so many outdoor opportunities."

In 2011, Steinhauser completed his eighth year of running all the Grand Prix races. He's still thankful for that fateful day he won entry into the Mount Marathon Race. It's still one of Evan's favorite races, "I like the Mount Marathon Race for the awesome tradition. Even after I reach the ten-year mark I plan on participating as long as my knees will let me."

Steinhauser can't help wondering what the Mountain Gods have in store for him in two years.

Colorful Men of the Mountain

A few playful athletes have run the race adorned with capes, wigs, horns, and feathers. In 1983 "Cowman" Ken Shirk from Hawaii ran the race wearing a ten-pound buffalo horn headpiece. Then "Crazy" Bill Carroll of Anchorage strapped on a hard-shelled Army helmet. A few years later "Elvis"—alias John Smith—made his entrance into the race wearing a wig, sunglasses, cape, and a blue rhinestone suit. But for pure audacity of costume, none come close to "The Birdman."

Brian Stoecker: Birdman

"Birdman! Birdman!" chants the crowd as Brian Stoecker performs his trademark pirouette at the bottom of the chute. Stoecker—feathered headdress fluttering in the breeze, war paint covering his face, bib number pinned to his nipple rings—is hard to overlook. Stoecker created his Birdman persona four years after he ran his first Mount Marathon Race in 1990. But look beneath the feathers and war paint and you'll find a man of many talents and zany characters. Depending on his mood, he can morph into a California actor, writer, videographer, or athlete.

Birdman Brian Stoecker performs his trademark pirouette at the bottom of the chute.

Since 1990, he has continued to improve his time in the Mount Marathon Race, culminating with a personal best finish in 48:42 in 2002, a mere two and a half minutes behind the winner.

Although Stoecker was an All-State wrestler at Service High School in Anchorage during the early 1980s, mountain climbing eclipsed all other sports after he summited

Rainbow Peak for the first time in 1984. "After reaching the first summit, I looked up and saw a rock formation that looked like a castle," Stoecker said. "So naturally I had to keep going until I scrambled to the top. The view was awesome."

From then on whenever he joined his family on fishing trips in Prince William Sound, he asked his dad to put him ashore. Stoecker would spend the day hiking mountain trails while his family caught fish to fill the freezer.

After college, Stoecker spent a few years in Santa Monica, California, working as a television actor. But after immersing himself in the California beach scene, Stoecker reevaluated his goals and returned to Alaska and the solace of the mountains.

Stoecker starts training for the Mount Marathon Race in January and by April he climbs four or five mountains a week. On solo training runs, Stoecker works out the plot for the great Alaska novel he's writing. In addition to writing the story, he plans on directing and acting in the video presentation.

Thunderous applause and shouts of encouragement follow Stoecker as he heads down Fourth Avenue and sprints toward the finish line. "I love the run; it's a race like no other in Alaska because of the enthusiasm of the Seward crowd," he said. Under the feathers and painted face, surrounded by adoring fans, Brian Stoecker feels good.

Senior Runners
Charlie Brown, Heinrich Gruber, and Corky Corthell

When forty-year-old Ed Vogel won the race in 1925 he was considered an aberration: old men don't run, much less, win races. Since then, fifty-, sixty-, and seventy-year-old men and women have competed in the event, breaking barriers and stereotypes about age and fitness.

Charlie Brown, Heinrich Gruber, and Corky Corthell, all in their seventies, have never won the race, but they have demonstrated that the thrill of competition has nothing to do with chronological age.

When asked about the secrets of their mountain running success, the men talk about cod liver oil, energy ratios, and supportive wives. Their spouses—Shirley, Emmy, and Carolyn—hike with them, drive them to mountain runs, massage sore muscles, and cheer as they cross the finish line. With a total of 160 married years among them, it adds up to a remarkable amount of support.

Gruber was the first man over sixty to set a sixty to sixty-nine age group record in 1990 in 1:03:39. Eleven years later, in 2001, he set the first seventy to seventy-nine age group record in 1:23:23. Gruber and his wife emigrated from Austria to Canada in 1958, and then moved to Alaska in 1964. The snow-covered mountains of Alaska reminded Gruber of his home in Austria. He started running at the age of fifty when his two sons ran track in high school. Instead of sitting in the car waiting for them to finish their workout, he ran with them. He attributes his mountain running success to having "climbing legs" and a daily dose of cod liver oil.

Brown started running after his retirement in 1995 at the age of sixty-five when his daughter Bonnie asked him to run a 5K race with her. He won an age group medal, and was hooked. By 2001 he'd logged one thousand running miles. Brown ran his first Mount Marathon Race in 1998, and in 2000, ran a personal best of 1:45:00 at the age of sixty-nine. Heart surgery in 2002 took Brown out of Mount Marathon competition, but he still climbs mountains with friends and competes in 5K runs.

Corthell considers himself an engineer, not an athlete. So when he entered his first Mount Marathon Race in 1998, he turned to science for help. He figured out how much energy it took to lift one pound of weight up a mountain, then made sure his weight was at the optimum level for climbing. He lost twenty-five pounds and on race day cut labels from his shorts and clipped his nails to minimize his weight. He ran a personal best at the age of seventy-three in 2003 when he crossed the finish line in 1:27:00.

Corthell ran six out of seven races in the Grand Prix Series (sponsored by Alaska Mountain Runners) in 2003, the first man over seventy to accomplish that goal. The running community acknowledged his accomplishments by presenting him with the Alaska Mountain Runners Inspirational Award at their annual awards banquet.

In 2009, the Mount Marathon Committee had to add a new eighty to eighty-nine age group category when eighty-year-old Corky finished the race in 1:52:59. He threw down the gauntlet to older runners. "I'd like to see more competition in my age group," he said.

Alaska Mountain Turtles

Author's note: I don't just write about the race, I also run it with the Alaska Mountain Turtles, as we call ourselves, five "sassy senior" women from Anchorage, Alaska, ages sixty-two to seventy. In spring of 2003 we joined together to support and encourage one another in our quest to stay fit and to train for mountain runs.

I've always loved to play in the mountains. Although I'd backpacked, hiked, and biked with my six sons, I didn't get involved in competitions until they were grown. After I started running in my fifties, I climbed Mount Kilimanjaro in Tanzania, trekked in the Himalayas, and hiked the Inca Trail. Then, in 1998, Charlie Brown asked me if I'd like to train for a Mount Marathon Race. I said yes. It sounded like a unique way to celebrate my sixtieth birthday. The experience was so exhilarating that I've done it every year since, with a personal best finish in 2:00:41 in 2000.

All the Turtles started running mountains after raising their families. Mary Hensel, seventy, has run ten Mount Marathon Races with a personal best finish in 1:52:23 in 2004. In 2008 she set a new record in the seventy to seventy-nine age group in 1:57:02.

Three of the Turtles ran personal bests during the 2006 Mount Marathon Race: Claudette Hixon, sixty-eight, in 2:05:00, Sandy Johnson, sixty-four, in 1:54:00, and the youngest of the group, sixty-two-year-old Barbara Abercrombie, in 1:46:00.

Calling ourselves "turtles" takes the pressure off during races. Wearing turtle logo socks and T-shirts, turtle earrings, and sporting turtle tattoos, we're hard to miss. The pure joy we feel in moving our bodies is enough to keep us climbing high. We call young, competitive runners "hares" because they run circles around us.

The Turtles prefer to test ourselves on short runs like Bird Ridge, Mount Alyeska, and Mount Marathon. Running Matanuska Peak, a fourteen-mile, 9,000-foot-elevation gain, or Crow Pass Crossing, a twenty-six mile mountain traverse doesn't fit our definition of fun. We may be slow, but we're not dumb.

Arctic Valley Road, outside of Anchorage, a steep six-mile climb to a ski lodge, is the site of the Turtles' winter workouts. Subzero temperatures, howling winds, or darkness don't dampen our enthusiasm for an uphill run at 9 A.M. in December. Training with friends is the way to go. First, hugs all around, followed by words of encouragement. Visiting is, of course, one of the two reasons for being together. While running and talking, the Turtles solve problems. We tackle big issues: Whether studded soles or ice grippers give better traction; how to keep hands warm at −10°F; and where will we go for breakfast.

Alaska Mountain Turtles: Millie Spezialy, Claudette Hixon, Sandy Johnson, Barbara Abercombie, and Mary Hensel.

Mountain Turtles follow the snow as it recedes up mountain trails in spring. Bird Ridge, a scramble over rocks and snow to the 3,500-foot summit, replaces Arctic Valley as a training site in May. Turtles, moving at a turtle pace, take our time to reach the top, and we have been known to stop and smell spring flowers. But the thrill of reaching the summit is worth it. As the words of a popular Carpenters song from the '70s goes: "We're on the top of the world looking down on creation." Eagles soar below, their white-tipped wings outstretched to catch a ride on air currents.

Some legendary Mount Marathon hares have made the one and a half mile downhill run in under eleven minutes. Turtles consider it an exceptional day if they can make it down the treacherous course in less than thirty-five.

During the Fourth of July race, it's easy to spot a Turtle. We're at the back of the pack laboring upward as younger athletes hop, jump, and slide down. We cheer the hares as they fly by. In turn, these elite competitors offer encouragement to the Turtles: "Looking good. You're almost there." They seem to understand that even though they're king of the mountain today, they're also TNTs: "Turtles in Training."

Faces Behind the Race
Directors, Committee Members, and Volunteers

The unsung heroes behind the Mount Marathon Race are the many Seward volunteers who work year-round to prepare for the Fourth of July race.

Karol Fink, Race Committee Member

Karol Fink had already served on the race committee for five years in 2007. "I love everything about the race and will be happy to do another five," she said. Although she works as a registered dietician in Anchorage, she owns a house in Seward and calls the small town home. She went on to express her thoughts and feelings about the race. "Seward folks feel ownership of the race. They created and nurtured it for almost a hundred years. It's always been a Fourth of July celebration and race for families and everyone, not just elite runners. "If you live in Seward you see the mountain every day and watch runners train for the race. Even non-racers ask me, 'When was the last time you went up the mountain?' People in Seward are really proud of Seward runners, whether they win or not.

"The biggest challenge is to make everybody happy, from town merchants and sponsors, volunteers, spectators, and runners. The biggest problem is that we have more people who want to run the race than we have spaces available because around 85 percent of the participants return to the race year after year," she explained. Since anyone who finishes the race can run again the next year, and the race is limited to three hundred and fifty runners in each senior division, getting into the race is difficult. To make it easier for elite runners to take part in the race, a new rule was enacted in 2003 that allowed invited runners to compete. The remaining slots, vacated by previous runners, are filled in a lottery system. If a runner's name isn't picked in the lottery, started in 2002, the only option left is for them to buy their way into the race on July third, when ten men's and ten women's bibs are auctioned off to the highest bidder.

Fink takes the first week of July off from work to focus on race preparations. Up early on race day, she manages to compete in the women's run between race committee chores and announcer's duties at the awards ceremony.

★ Fit and Healthy for Life ★

As I crossed the finish line of the Tinker Belle half marathon in Disneyland in January 2013, the young woman beside me asked, "Do you mind telling me how old you are?" When I answered, she said, "I hope I can still be participating in runs when I'm seventy-five. You're my hero."

When I started running at the age of forty-six, after friends encouraged me to enter a 5K fun run, I never expected to be anyone's hero. But I enjoyed the comrade ship of the running community and sought out new running challenges. By the age of sixty I was winning age group medals and still getting faster. Older athletes in Alaska and around the world continue to shatter perceptions about age and fitness. Corky Corthell ran Mount Marathon at the age of eighty-two; Joe Redington Sr. completed the Iditarod 1,049-mile sled-dog race at the age of seventy-nine. Dick Griffith finished the last section of his epic Arctic journey on foot from Barter Island to Repulse Bay in 2000, at the age of seventy-three. The "Dipsea Demon," Jack Kirk, ran the Dipsea Race sixty-seven times between the ages of twenty-three and ninety-five.

As a youngster growing up in the 1940s I never worried about fitness; it just came naturally. My siblings and I spent many hours a day outside. We ran, walked, sledded, skated, climbed trees, played hide and seek, chopped and carried wood, and played softball. Work and play and a diet of fresh garden vegetables, wild berries, and small portions of meat (one chicken fed our family of eleven) kept us fit and at a healthy weight.

Raising six sons in Alaska kept me busy for the next few years. I took my sons outside every day. We walked, skied, skated, hiked, played tennis, and backpacked. Family picnics always included a wild game of volleyball.

After turning fifty I noticed that if I took a few weeks off from running it was harder to get going again. Reading my way through health and nutrition books I discovered that we lose muscle tone, aerobic capacity, and flexibility as we age. But there was an antidote to aging: exercise.

I joined the local YMCA and began working out with weights three times a week to maintain muscle strength; I ski, bicycle, and hike to maintain a healthy endurance level; and attend yoga sessions to tone muscles, increase flexibility, and relieve stress. I never give myself permission to say no when it's time to head to the gym, no matter how comfortable the easy chair. After noticing the new bounce in my step my husband joined me during workouts at the Y.

You too have a choice. It's never too late to set and implement fitness goals. Reach out and savor each new day. After all the best is yet to come.

She arrived in Seward in the summer of 1995, and ran her first Mount Marathon Race two years later, finishing eighteenth in 1:09:00. A competitive soccer player from third grade through college, Fink now runs, bikes, weight trains, and attends spinning classes at a health club to stay fit.

In the twelve years from 1997 to 2008 that Fink has run the Mount Marathon Race, her finish time has varied by only seven minutes. She posted a personal best in 2007 in 1:02:00 to grab fourth place. "I want to do well for Seward to make people proud. I don't set goals—I just want to do as well as I can."

Kathy Bingman, Race Codirector with Rich Houghton

After serving on the race committee for five years, Bingman became codirector of the race with Rich Houghton from 2001 to 2003. They decided to split the job when they found out how much work was involved.

Kathy Bingman, race codirector.

"I watched the Mount Marathon Race for twenty years before I ran it in 1991. It quickly became one of my favorites," said Kathy Bingman. She's run the race fifteen times and set a fifty to fifty-nine age group record in 2000 in 1:13:40.

Bingman moved to Seward from California with her baby daughter, Surya—which means sunshine in Hindu—in 1971 seeking a simpler lifestyle. With finances tight, Bingman rented a small cabin and used the creek to wash out the baby's diapers. "I made many friends in the community and it was a great place to raise kids. You see the cycle of life, from birth to death."

As part of a healthy lifestyle, Bingman eats organic, runs, swims, bikes, and practices yoga. She qualified for the Boston Marathon in 2000, but sprained an ankle four weeks before the event and couldn't compete. She'd already completed eight marathons in eight different states, ran Crow Pass Crossing in 1999, and competed in all sixteen Lost Lake Runs. "Being surrounded by so much beauty on the Lost Lake Run is awesome. I feel like I have wings on my feet," she said.

Bingman was in the midst of chemotherapy for breast cancer in the spring of 1998, when her only daughter, Surya, was killed in a car accident on her way to Seward for a practice run on Mount Marathon.

"Surya was my best friend. She ran her first race in 1994, after I got the bug to run the race. Once I took her up the mountain on her first practice run, she was hooked. Although she was slower than me in her first couple of races, she got faster each year. Surya's time and position improved each of the four years she did the race, moving up from thirty-fourth in 1994 in 1:21:57 to seventeenth in 1997 in 1:08:35. Surya's goal was to place tenth in the 1998 run. After her death I planned to walk the race and take her bib with me. But on July second I sliced my finger and asked Karol Fink to carry Surya's bib behind hers." With an enigmatic smile Bingman added, "Karol finished tenth."

Surya Borg improved her time each of the four years she ran the race.

During Bingman and Houghton's tenure as race codirectors, their goal was to give credit to more runners. They also enacted a change in bib procedure. The top fifty bibs were to be given out to runners in the order of their finishes the previous year.

Bingman commented about her running philosophy: "I plan on staying healthy and hope to run the race as long as possible. I want my body to go where my mind wants to go. Climbing a mountain is like life: one step at a time will get you where you want to go."

Chuck Echard, Race Director

"After innocently offering a few race suggestions in 1978, I was handed the director's job. I was it, the race director and committee." Chuck Echard went on to comment: "This race is not just about runners, it's about all the people who watch the run from their boats and on the street."

As race director, Echard initiated a limit of two hundred runners for each of the race categories for safety reasons. And he was the first race director to gather statistics for press releases. He became the resident historian, gathering all the old records and compiling them into three volumes for posterity.

After his five-year tenure as race director, Echard took on the job of timing the event. "The race is exciting, addicting. That's why I decided to stay involved."

Lori Draper, Perennial Race Committee Member

"My husband and I got involved in the race in 1978 when we became the timers for the run. We made our own paper bibs with magic marker pens and timed with two stopwatches, a legal pad, and pencils. Awards were presented right after the race in front of the Yukon Bar. Life was simpler back then.

"To keep 'bandits'—runners without bibs—from doing the race and messing up our timing, we enacted a new rule. If we catch someone running without a bib number they have to work five years as a volunteer."

Still involved as a committee member, Draper commented, "It's like we're caretakers of this race—we want to keep the integrity intact. And besides that, it's a lot of fun."

Jean Cripps, Longtime Volunteer

Although hundreds of Seward folks volunteer for the race year after year, Jean Cripps name comes up again and again as an extraordinary volunteer.

Jean Cripps and her husband were a military family who went fishing in Seward in 1966 and decided it was the place they wanted to live after retiring. "Our oldest son is handicapped and he loved to fish, and the Seward people were so laid-back and accepting." Both jumped into community jobs and volunteer work in 1977, after settling in Seward.

Two years later Cripps started her long tenure as a Mount Marathon volunteer. Her first job was to give first aid to injured runners at the bottom of the cliffs. By 1983 she'd switched to working triage at the finish line. "I look at a runner's face to tell me if he needs help," Cripps said. "We had an ambulance at the finish to take injured runners to the hospital if needed. Both triage and ambulance services were free to racers. The first years we didn't even have a tent to place injured runners; we just laid blankets on the sidewalk and worked on them there. The most common job I did at the finish line was cleaning out dirt and picking stones out of abrasions and cuts."

Besides her work as a volunteer nurse at the Mount Marathon Race, Cripps has been a member of the all-volunteer Seward Ambulance Corps for more than twenty-five years. Both she and her husband have worked and taught nursing in Seward, and her husband was mayor from 1981 to 1985. Although a knee replacement in 2007 forced Cripps to withdraw as a volunteer, she still stood at the finish line, with the aid of a cane, and passed out words of encouragement.

Tom Welsh and the Top of the Mountain Crew

Tom Welsh has headed a team of volunteers stationed at the top of Mount Marathon since 1997. Buster Bryant, Dennis Magnuson, and Bob Bingman round out this team of dedicated timers at the halfway point of the race.

Welsh arrived in Alaska in 1993 to work in the oil fields and within a year bought a house in Seward. "My wife and I like the small town culture and enjoy sailing our boat in Resurrection Bay."

After watching the Fourth of July race for two years, Welsh and his friend Bryant ran the race in 1995, finishing in a respectable 1:26:00 and 1:28:00, respectively.

They chose not to run the race in 1997, but still wanted to be part of the fun, so they decided to volunteer. The first year saw them at the finish line, grabbing bib numbers. A year later Welsh asked the race director, "Do you need anyone at the top of the mountain?" They did, and he's held the job ever since.

On the morning of the race the timers pick up gear at 6:30 A.M., strap on their backpacks, and by 8:00 A.M. are hiking to the top.

A few minutes before the start of the women and men's races, Welsh makes radio contact with volunteers at the start line and they all turn on the timing clocks simultaneously. As a runner rounds the rock at the top of the mountain, a timer calls out the runner's bib number, and another records the time. "We use the radio to call the finish line when the top runners reach the top. We also use the radios to call for help when runners are injured on the mountain."

Bryant said he matches names to bib numbers so he can cheer the runners as they round the halfway point, "'Betty, from Wasilla. Barney, from Anchorage.' Hearing their name called out usually brings a smile to their face," he said.

Timers stay at their post until the last runner rounds the rock at the top, around five o'clock But sometimes it's longer. One year the crew started down at five only to see a man still laboring up. Welsh called out, "Anybody behind you?" With sweat pouring off his chin, the man replied, "Yeah, my dad." Since the

Tom Welsh and his volunteer crew at the top of the mountain.

In 2008, the race timing procedure was updated with the introduction of electronic timing chips. Welsh and his crew are still stationed at the top to check numbers and to be sure runners cross the timing mat.

timers are also the sweepers, the team didn't get off the mountain until 7:30 P.M.

Welsh and his team are enthusiastic about their job at the top of the mountain, "We have the best view in town, and most of the athletes are happy to see us."

Dave Squire, Fire Chief

"As the number of competitors in the Mount Marathon Race grew, fire department personnel and volunteer rescue workers started seeing more serious injuries. It was evident that we needed professional mountain rescue training. Since 1986, the fire department has spent the month of June on Mount Marathon training for mountain rescue," said Fire Chief Dave Squire. Then he added, "In 1987 an avalanche dropped lots of snow in the chute, creating an ice cave, and we were fearful that a runner could fall forty feet if he broke through the surface. We set up ropes before the race to help with rescue operations. Three people needed help when they fell. It ended the race for them because runners are disqualified if someone helps them during the race."

Besides helping injured runners down the mountain on the Fourth of July, the department also rescues tourists and hikers off the mountain two or three times a year. Two weeks after the 2008 Mount Marathon Race, a woman too scared to climb down Mount Marathon was helped off the mountain after an eight-hour rescue effort by the Seward Volunteer Fire Department, the Alaska Mountain Rescue Group, and the Alaska State Troopers.

Steve Lemme, Auctioneer

"The first Mount Marathon Auction in 1995 was a pretty laid-back affair," said Steve Lemme, auctioneer and Seward resident. "It was held on the street in front of the Yukon Bar and the highest price paid for a bib was $185. But the law of supply and demand kept pushing the bib price higher and higher. By 1996 the top price for a bib had risen to $275 and by 2008 to over $1,100. Each auction is unique. I like to watch rivalry bidding and have seen many different strategies used in the bidding war. Some bidders overextend their bank accounts, and family and friends chip in to make up the difference."

Lemme, a professional auctioneer, arrived in Seward in 1984 looking for business and professional opportunities. "It's a very caring community. People here are quick to lend a helping hand to someone who's down on their luck."

After Lemme helps put up the bandstand on race day, he dons a chef's hat and barbecues chicken for the Catholic community's annual fund-raiser. A musician and songwriter, Lemme formed a band after arriving in Seward and recently released a CD of original spiritual songs.

7

2012—
A Year to Remember

Mount Marathon demands respect from casual day hikers and competitive racers alike. For almost one hundred years racers have survived and flourished during race day. That changed in 2012 when one racer was lost and two were seriously injured.

Search and Rescue Operation on Mount Marathon

No one expected to lose a man. Runners in the 2012 Mount Marathon race expected a few cuts and bruises. But no one ever vanishes into thin air.

The men's race started at 3 P.M. Forty-four minutes and seven seconds later Matt Novakovich crossed the finish line. Only 11 of 365 racers took more than two hours to complete the course. The last man crossed the finish line in 2:57:13.

By 6 P.M. all racers were accounted for except Michael LeMaitre. Race officials weren't too concerned, because LeMaitre told his family that he'd take longer than most to make the round-trip.

At 9 P.M. LeMaitre's family reported him overdue.

Volunteer timekeepers who were descending from the summit after an eight-hour shift reported seeing LeMaitre about 200 feet from the top. He was three hours into the race, in last place, and moving up the mountain slowly.

"There's no one timing at the top. The race is over," a volunteer called out. "Why not go down with us?"

According to a Chamber of Commerce representative, LeMaitre told the lead timer he wanted to keep going. Like many athletes LeMaitre probably figured he was close to the top and wanted to complete the entire race course. A light rain was falling, but due to the long daylight hours in Alaska during June and July, visibility was still good.

LeMaitre's athletic background was similar to many other older racers: he wasn't racing to be in the top one hundred. He was there for the experience. LeMaitre was a community readiness consultant who worked at the Family Support Center in Anchorage. He came to Alaska in 1966 and embraced an active lifestyle, including sailing, hiking, cross-country skiing, and kayaking.

LeMaitre had completed the ultra-sports event, Iditaski, a long-distance ski race. Only racers who know their abilities, level of experience, and the amount of risk involved are allowed to participate. The overall philosophy of ultra-sports events is that if race organizers offer too much support, you cheat the true adventurers out of a big part of why they are on the trail.

LeMaitre had accomplished many of his athletic goals, but he wanted to run the Mount Marathon Race. Year after year he put his name into the lottery and was overjoyed when his name was drawn in March 2012.

As a rookie, sixty-six-year-old LeMaitre was required to attend a mandatory safety meeting the night prior to the race. First-time racers view a slide show that reviews the race route and possible problem areas. They are told that if they have not been up the mountain they should not be in the race. LeMaitre had never been up the mountain.

A picture of LeMaitre, taken near the start of the race, shows him wearing a big smile, black shorts and T-shirt, and a black headband.

Many hours later, after hearing that a racer was still on the mountain, Dave Squire, City of Seward fire chief, organized a search party. Volunteers called out LeMaitre's name as they fanned out along the race route. Their only response: an ominous silence.

An air search was begun the first night by an Alaska State Trooper

Helo-1 helicopter using FLIR, a heat-sensing camera. When LeMaitre wasn't found by morning Alaska State Troopers put out a call for more volunteers from organized search and rescue teams in Anchorage.

Members of the Alaska Mountain Rescue Group (AMRG) were called at 5 A.M. to help in the search, particularly the technical terrain higher on the mountain. Initial teams were on the road within an hour and arrived in Seward by 8 A.M. Additional volunteers from Alaska Search and Rescue Dogs, BARK-9, and the Anchorage Nordic Ski Patrol were requested later that morning. They were joined by volunteers from Matanuska Search and Rescue, National Park Service, Air National Guard, and Bear Creek Fire Station.

By noon on July 5, Alaska State Troopers and AMRG had set up an incident command post at the Civil Air Patrol building in Seward. AMRG's job was to integrate all the volunteer organizations into search teams. Dave Squire, representing the City of Seward, coordinated local volunteers from Seward for an integrated search effort.

An AMRG Operation Section Chief, Dean Knapp, left Eagle River at 1 P.M. and arrived in Seward mid-afternoon. "I stopped at Summit Lodge to call and see if LeMaitre had been located," he said. "I expected to hear that he'd been found."

Meanwhile, the search management team was working on a detailed plan for coordinating the search effort. Since half the mountain portion of the race route is thick with trees and the other half is above tree line, the key to managing the search effort is to clearly define and segment the search areas. Search and rescue teams were assigned to high probability sites.

The search management team used a color-coded 3-D satellite map that divided areas of highest likelihood of finding LeMaitre. Red-coded areas were given highest priority. These search areas turned out to be the most difficult to penetrate because of thick growths of alder trees, devil's club, and numerous ferns and ground plants.

"The undergrowth was so thick, we couldn't see someone twenty feet away," said Brian Aho from AMRG.

Members of a search and rescue crew study topographical maps of Mount Marathon in their efforts to locate a missing runner.

After another twenty-four hours passed without finding a single clue to LeMaitre's location, doubts began to plague volunteers. "It keeps me awake at night," said Allyson Youngblood, AMRG member.

Weather and terrain were big problems. Over the next few days a steady rain fell, turning an already slick trail into a muddy mire. "I had crampons on my feet and an ice ax in my hand and still slid six feet down the mountain," said Brian Aho from AMRG. "It was almost impossible to stay on my feet," he added.

Three more helicopters joined the search. The 212th Air National Guard sent a Pave Hawk helicopter the next day. A second Trooper helicopter and a Robinson R44, from a Seward air flight service, were also utilized in search efforts. Each carried a trained spotter.

Five search dogs and their handlers, from Alaska Search and Rescue Dogs and BARK-9, all trained in wilderness and avalanche search, cadaver retrieval, and tracking, were also used in the search. Rain continued to be a problem, making it impossible for the dogs to find a scent.

Dean Knapp commented, "I didn't shut down the radios until 2:00 A.M. and we were online again at 6 A.M." Rescue personnel on the mountain had a stand-alone radio system and reported back to mission headquarters. They found a child's backpack, a few gloves, and an aluminum water bottle, none of which belonged to LeMaitre. Every footprint or potential clue found was reported back to command post.

After three days, frustration showed in the fatigued faces of the search teams. Search and Rescue volunteers from Anchorage logged 900 hours on the mountain, and Seward Fire Department teams another 1,100. And still no clue was found as to LeMaitre's whereabouts. When rescue crews aren't successful, they keep reassessing. "If only we had..."

After conferring with the family on July 8, Alaska State Troopers called off the official search. But Seward Fire Department continued a more limited search with local resources for a few additional days.

At the request of the Alaska State Troopers, a dog rescue team from BARK-9 and one AMRG member were on the mountain again on November 3, 2012. The underbrush was still a problem. "The vegetation is still too thick to search effectively," they reported.

The unthinkable happened. Michael LeMaitre is still missing. The mission will remain open until he is found.

The Healing Power of Love

An accident happened during the 2012 Mount Marathon Race, changing forever the lives of the Kenney Family.

Veteran racer Matt Kenney slipped and tumbled down the rocks, sustaining a trauma to the head, a broken leg, and numerous cuts and bruises. He had traversed the same area many times without incident. It would take the love of his family and friends to restore him to health.

Kenney loved to participate in sports, from flying down a ski hill to playing a bone-crunching football game. His gridiron skills earned him a football scholarship to St. Mary of the Plains in Dodge City, Kansas. As a freshman, Kenney helped his team win the Kansas Collegiate Athletic Conference Championship. Two years later, after suffering a knee injury on a ski run, Kenney went looking for a new sport.

Biking was a passion he shared with his kids, plus hikes up Flattop Mountain in the spring and fall. Kenney's dogs, Rubye, a beagle, and Jackson, a yellow Lab, accompanied him on longer mountain hikes.

Many folks scoffed at the sight of the small beagle at Kenney's side, but it was if the dog were made for mountain hikes. Rubye climbed purposefully, staying on the trail and kept a steady pace even when snow blanketed the route.

In 2004 Kenney and his dogs were sitting on the tailgate of his pickup at the Bird Ridge trailhead when Brad Precosky and Barney Griffith sauntered over and asked him if he'd like to join their Sunday training runs. He recognized them from newspaper accounts of their successful Mount Marathon careers. Smiling broadly, he accepted their offer. "Running mountains became Kenney's passion, plus the friendships," said Barney Griffiths.

After hearing the excitement in runners' voices as they swapped tall tales of their Mount Marathon experiences, Kenney thought he'd give the race a go. But he wasn't willing to buy his way into it. After putting his name into the lottery for the third time his name was picked in 2005.

"Being able to train and race with his friends meant the world to Matt," his wife, Gretchen, said, "He was a warrior and this mountain was his battle each and every year. He was always very modest of his accomplishments and would rather tell about his friends' achievements."

Kenney ran a personal best in 2007 with his finish in 55:15. But he knew that he wouldn't get faster because of past injuries to his knee, so he chose to enjoy the runs and take in the moments with his friends.

Year after year Kenney's family stood at the same location on Jefferson Street so his children could touch their dad's hand as he ran by. In 2012, Kenney's family expected to see him about an hour after the race started. When he didn't appear Gretchen called to ask her friend Brad Precosky,

"Have you seen Matt?"

"No, but I'll check on him," Precosky promised.

Gretchen hurried to the finish line to ask race officials about her husband. "Bib number 46 was taken to the hospital," an official told her. Forty-six was Kenney's bib number. Trying to control her panic, Gretchen headed toward a state trooper's car.

"I didn't even know where the hospital was," she said. The trooper told the Kenney family to get in the car and he drove them to the hospital.

Brad Precosky and his partner, Romny Dodd, stayed with the children while Gretchen rushed to the hospital trauma room. She paced the hallway until she was allowed to see him. "He looked like he'd been dipped in mud and rolled in rocks and leaves. He was hooked up to machines and blood was everywhere. Although he was unresponsive I talked to him as they prepared to medevac him to Anchorage. The plane was too small for me to go with Matt so my friends drove the children and me to Anchorage. The 130-mile ride from Seward was agony. I got sick and threw up."

The Anchorage running community wrapped its arms around the Kenney family, keeping vigil with Gretchen at the hospital.

"We have always been the ones who donate, raise money, and volunteer our hours. I have never been on the receiving end of a community coming together in time of need. It was humbling to have others raise money for us, to have strangers mow our lawn. And bring meals and groceries every week. Someone even donated an airplane ticket for my niece to come to Alaska to care for the kids. I don't know where I would be emotionally, financially, and spiritually if I did not have the support of the community."

One of Kenney's mountain running buddies, Barney Griffith, decided to show solidarity with Kenney, who kept his head shaved, by shaving his own head. Brad Precosky and Keith Weinhold quickly agreed to join him. Kenney's good friend Matt Novakovich hesitated. "I'd better ask Tiffany [his wife] first," he said. She gave her consent, and the four friends took the plunge and went hairless.

Precosky and Dodd kept the long vigil with Gretchen during the two weeks Kenney was in the intensive care unit. After Kenney was transferred to a medical floor, volunteers took turns sitting with Kenney while Gretchen took short breaks to deal with her job or to be with her children.

The first visit from Kenney's children, Justin, twelve, and Savannah, nine, took place on July 14. "Although Matt couldn't speak or barely open his eyes, he turned his head to the sounds of their voices," Gretchen said. "It was the most movement that he had made in the past ten days."

The children visited their dad again, prior to his transfer to Denver, Colorado. The crowd in the hospital room erupted with cheers when Savannah reached over to kiss her father and he responded by moving his cheek toward her and puckering his lips. "I kissed him twelve more times and he did the same thing," Savannah said, beaming. All in the room were amazed at the power of love to reach into Matt's injured brain.

On July 30 Kenney was transferred by air medical transport to Craig Hospital in Englewood. This time Gretchen was able to go with Kenney but became claustrophobic in the small space and needed to be medicated.

"Dr. Alan Weintraub was just who Matt needed," said Gretchen, about the neurologist who cared for Kenney at Craig Hospital. It was at Craig that Kenney spoke for the first time. "Give me a kiss," he said in response to Gretchen's declaration of love.

Kenney's best friend, Steve Parrish, flew down for a quick visit and Gretchen's family came to provide support.

"Because Matt was in great physical shape, it helped in his recovery," Gretchen said. After a pause, she added, "Matt's resting heart rate was forty before the accident." Gretchen stayed with Matt the first three weeks he was in Colorado, only returning to Anchorage for the Alyeska Mountain Run, a fund-raiser for Kenney.

"I wish he were home," Griffith said. "He's been a big part of my life for the past five years. During the winter we climb Bird Ridge together two days a week. Safety was always a priority for Matt. He was an excellent downhill runner, very sure on his feet."

On October 24 Kenney was moved to a rehabilitation center in Omaha, Nebraska. "The first day they had him walk all day," Gretchen said.

The family traveled to Nebraska for the Thanksgiving weekend. "It was the first time we were able to go out to dinner as a family since July 3. Kenney tired easily so we limited our activities. The best part was that Savannah got to show her dad some new gymnastic moves and Justin enjoyed just sitting next to his father. Every now and then he would lean over and hug his dad. It was very enjoyable and therapeutic for all of us," Gretchen said.

In January Kenney's family was overjoyed to find out that Kenney was coming home in March to continue his recovery with his family. "Matt's physical body is fully healed and he's already talking about hiking Rainbow Trail near Anchorage with his friends and dogs. He still has moments of confusion but is making steady progress in short-term memory,' said Gretchen

Love comes in many forms, love of challenge, love of work, love of family and friends. Kenney is a passionate and loving man who savors life, and although participating in one of his loves left him injured, his other loves blanketed him with care. Gretchen and their children are anxious to have him back home. His running buddies look forward to the day he can rejoin them in the mountains. His coworkers at K & L Distributors, who donated 500 hours of vacation time, look forward to his return. Matt Kenney is a lucky man.

National Guard Pilot Penny Assman Takes a Fall

Emergency medical technicians (EMT) position themselves at the bottom of the cliffs near the base of Mount Marathon. It's where most accidents happen. Competitive runners push themselves hard on the uphill section of the race and by the time they reach the cliffs on the downhill route, they're exhausted.

Penny Assman had a big goal for her first Mount Marathon Race. She hoped for a top three finish. She was right on schedule when she reached the top of the cliffs, but after taking the wrong fork in the trail found herself sliding out of control down the rock face.

Lucky for her, volunteer EMT Autumn Ludwig, from the Bear Creek Volunteer Fire Department, saw Assman's downward flight and instinctively held out her arms. Although Ludwig broke Assman's fall, Assman hit hard as they both slammed to the ground. After being stabilized and placed on a gurney, Assman was taken by ambulance to Seward Hospital.

A medevac helicopter flew her to Providence Hospital in Anchorage after Seward Hospital staff evaluated her injuries. As captain in the Utah Guard and commander of her medevac helicopter unit, Assman had flown many rescue missions. This time she was the one needing help.

Assman, thirty-four, suffered three broken ribs on her right side and a lacerated liver. People in prime physical condition heal faster and Assman was no exception. She was up and walking by July 7 and released from the hospital two days later. Within a week of her fall, she was able to thank Autumn Ludwig in person for her help. Assman knew that if Ludwig hadn't broken her fall she could have sustained even worse injuries.

But Assman was worried. She was well aware of the rule stating racers must finish the race to be eligible to run again the following year. Since she didn't finish the race, Assman was afraid she couldn't compete in 2013. The Chamber director assured Assman that she had a legitimate reason for not crossing the finish line and would be able to run the following year.

Striving for excellence has been Assman's goal for most of her life. Although she served two tours in Iraq in 2009 and 2010, she says the biggest challenge she's had to deal with was the two months of convalescence. No working out at the gym and cutting back on other activities.

Assman plans on running the race in 2013. She commented to an *Anchorage Daily News* reporter, "As odd as it is to say, I think now I have a chip on my shoulder." Then she added, "Mount Marathon 1, Penny 0. Next year it's going to be Mount Marathon 1, Penny 1. I just want to even the score."

Race Rules and Annual Winners

How to Apply

Mount Marathon Race Application Process
The Mount Marathon Race application process begins on January 1 of each year and runs through March 31. Applicants apply online at Seward.com. Applications received after midnight, March 31 (Alaska Time Zone) will not be considered. The final runners list is posted on the Seward.com website in April.

Entry Fees
Entry fees are due at the time the application is submitted. Payment is made during the application process using PayPal services.
* Junior Race: $25 ($5 refundable if unsuccessful in lottery)
* Senior Race: $65 ($10 refundable if unsuccessful in lottery)
* Entry fees are waived for past champions of the senior races. (Fees may change over time. Please check the website for current race registration fees.)

Eligibility
Junior race entrants must be at least seven years old and under age eighteen on July Fourth. Senior race entrants must be at least age eighteen on July Fourth. If any entrant falsifies any information on the application form, such as age or race category (junior or senior), the entrant will be subject to disqualification. Women may not run in the men's race and men may not run in the women's race.

Proposed Rule Changes in 2013

The Seward Chamber of Commerce and the Mount Marathon Race committee are looking for ways to allow new runners into the race. To keep priority status, a senior runner must finish within the first 225 runners across the finish line or finish with the top ten in their age group.

In 2013, the available slots for each division will be filled as follows:
* Previous winners of the men's or women's race.
* First 225 finishers from the 2012 race in each division.
* Top ten finishers from each age group.
* Veteran racers (those who have finished ten nonconsecutive senior races).
* 2012 registered runners who were unable to run but received official waiver status.
* Junior runners who finished the race the previous year and have aged into the senior race.
* Special invitations.
* Runners selected through the lottery process.

Given the serious injuries and the tragic death that occurred during the 2012 race, the Seward Chamber of Commerce issued the following rule changes to the Official Rules of Conduct:
* Senior racers must cross past the junior race point (halfway up the mountain) within one hour.
* Junior racers must cross by the Squirrels' Inn within thirty minutes of start time.

Lottery

First-time (rookie) and non-priority applicants for all divisions (junior and senior) are allocated the remaining slots through a lottery process. The lottery will take place at the Seward Chamber of Commerce during the first full week of April and results will be posted on the website April 18. Odds change each year based on the total number of applications received.

Auction and Raffle

Due to popular demand, additional race slots are offered through auction and raffle activities. Individuals who receive a slot through the auction, raffle, or junior drawing are eligible for priority status provided they complete their race. The activities take place at 7 P.M. on July 3, prior to the mandatory safety meeting. The auction and lottery are open to all individuals: those applicants not selected in the lottery are eligible to participate as well as individuals that did not previously apply. Individuals participating in the auction and raffle must be present and cannot designate another individual to participate in their stead. Payment is required immediately and may be made by cash or credit card.

Ten race slots are auctioned off for each of the races. Competition for the bibs has grown more competitive each year. High bid for a man's bib in 2011 was $2,400, and high bid for women was $1,400. The average price for both men and women was somewhat lower, but any runner who hopes to buy a bib in the auction had better start a savings account and get a second job. Prior to the auction, one additional senior race slot is drawn raffle-style for the senior race. Tickets for the raffle may be purchased for $5 each at the auction site prior to the event.

Ten junior names are drawn at random for the junior race. Juniors must be present and sign up with the drawing coordinator prior to 7 P.M.

Special Invitations

Winners of one of the Alaska Mountain Runners Grand Prix Series are eligible to participate in the following year's Mount Marathon Race by special invitation.

In rare instances, the Mount Marathon Race Committee grants one-year invitations to applicants for special circumstances such as documented outstanding results in other mountain races or other justifying conditions.

For more information about the race check out the Seward.com website and click on News and Events.

Top 100 Times on Mount Marathon

1	Bill Spencer	0:43:21	1981		34	Ben Ward	0:45:56	2012
2	Tobias Schwoerer	0:43:39	2004		35	Bill Spencer	0:45:59	1982
3	Trond Flagstad	0:44:03	2008		36	Sam Hill	0:45:59	2008
4	Matt Novakovich	0:44:07	2012		37	Bill Spencer	0:46:01	1983
5	Bill Spencer	0:44:11	1974		38	Brent Knight	0:46:02	2006
6	Jonathan Chaffee	0:44:25	1968		39	Matias Saari	0:46:04	2011
7	Bill Spencer	0:44:25	1976		40	Brad Precosky	0:46:10	1999
8	Trond Flagstad	0:44:26	2012		41	Matias Saari	0:46:10	2010
9	Jonathan Chaffee.	0:44:28	1967		42	Tor Christopherson	0:46:11	2012
10	Bill Spencer	0:44:37	1975		43	Brad Precosky	0:46:14	2007
11	Trond Flagstad	0:44:40	2010		44	Bill Spencer	0:46:15	1991
12	Eric Strabel	0:44:40	2011		45	Jeff Johnson	0:46:17	1979
13	Sam Young	0:44:49	1985		46	Todd Boonstra	0:46:17	1998
14	Brent Knight	0:44:58	2011		47	Brad Precosky	0:46:17	2002
15	Tom Besh	0:44:59	1977		48	Michael Graham	0:46:24	1988
16	Brad Precosky	0:45:07	2001		49	Brad Precosky	0:46:24	2005
17	Bill Spencer	0:45:08	1985		50	Brent Knight	0:46:24	2010
18	Matias Saari	0:45:13	2012		51	Trond Flagstad	0:46:26	2007
19	Gene Morgan	0:45:16	1972		52	Brent Knight	0:46:28	2012
20	Todd Boonstra	0:45:17	1997		53	Bill Spencer	0:46:29	1977
21	Brian Bethard	0:45:17	2005		54	Ben Ward	0:46:29	2010
22	Mark Iverson	0:45:18	2011		55	Jim Renkert	0:46:33	1987
23	Brad Precosky	0:45:31	2000		56	Brad Precosky	0:46:33	2004
24	Jeff Johnson	0:45:32	1976		57	Clint McCool	0:46:33	2005
25	Sam Young	0:45:32	1986		58	Jeff Johnson	0:46:35	1980
26	Bill Spencer	0:45:32	1986		59	Tom Besh	0:46:36	1969
27	Brad Precosky	0:45:42	2006		60	Gene Morgan	0:46:40	1973
28	Eric Strabel	0:45:42	2010		61	Jim Renkert	0:46:40	1981
29	Brian Bethard	0:45:47	2004		62	Mark Iverson	0:46:41	2012
30	Tom Besh	0:45:49	1973		63	John Roynor	0:46:42	1977
31	Trond Flagstad	0:45:52	2005		64	Clint McCool	0:46:42	2006
32	Tom Besh	0:45:53	1967		65	Matias Saari	0:46:42	2008
33	Trond Flagstad	0:45:54	2006		66	Matt Novakovich	0:46:44	2011

Race Rules and Annual Winners

67	Jeff Johnson	0:46:46	1978		84	Clint McCool	0:47:07	2004
68	Marten Martensen	0:46:49	1995		85	Jens Beck	0:47:07	2008
69	Brent Knight	0:46:50	2007		86	Barney Griffith	0:47:09	2001
70	Eric Strabel	0:46:52	2001		87	Brad Precosky	0:47:13	1997
71	Eric Strabel	0:46:52	2012		88	Barney Griffith	0:47:13	2006
72	Marten Martensen	0:46:54	1992		89	Andrew Liebner	0:47:13	2010
73	Darin Markwardt	0:46:54	2001		90	Todd Boonstra	0:47:16	2002
74	Barney Griffith	0:46:54	2005		91	Eric Strabel	0:47:16	2004
75	William Spencer	0:46:55	1964		92	Robert Whitney	0:47:16	2011
76	Marten Martensen	0:46:55	1997		93	Guy Thibodeau	0:47:17	1977
77	Dale Shea	0:46:57	1970		94	Steve Buchanan	0:47:17	1993
78	Eric Strabel	0:46:57	2002		95	Eli Lane	0:47:17	2000
79	William Spencer	0:46:59	1967		96	Mike Kramer	0:47:18	2006
80	Barney Griffith	0:46:59	2004		97	Darin Markwardt	0:47:21	2010
81	Sam Hill	0:46:59	2007		98	Marten Martensen	0:47:23	1998
82	Brad Precosky	0:46:59	2008		99	Todd Boonstra	0:47:23	2004
83	Trond Flagstad	0:47:06	2004		100	Matt Adams	0:47:23	2006

Top 88 Times on Mount Marathon
Women Under 60 minutes

1	Nancy Pease	0:50:30	1990		15	Nancy Pease	0:53:06	1991
2	Carmen Young	0:50:54	1986		16	Lynn Salaries	0:53:19	1983
3	Nancy Pease	0:51:13	1989		17	Patti Foldager	0:53:22	1991
4	Nancy Pease	0:51:41	1992		18	Kikkan Randall	0:53:29	2010
5	Cedar Bourgeois	0:51:44	2005		19	Nancy Pease	0:53:50	1995
6	Cedar Bourgeois	0:51:48	2010		20	Carmen Young	0:53:53	1988
7	Holly Brooks	0:51:53	2012		21	Deborah Nordyke	0:53:55	1991
8	Holly Brooks	0:51:58	2010		22	Nancy Pease	0:54:09	1984
9	Kikkan Randall	0:52:03	2011		23	Cedar Bourgeois	0:54:19	2009
10	Cedar Bourgeois	0:52:11	2008		24	Nina Kemppel	0:54:20	2000
11	Carmen Young	0:52:15	1987		25	Nancy Pease	0:54:45	1986
12	Holly Brooks	0:52:22	2011		26	Lauren Fritz	0:54:47	2012
13	Cedar Bourgeois	0:52:33	2006		27	Nina Kemppel	0:55:04	2002
14	Carmen Young	0:52:58	1990		28	Laura Brosius	0:55:04	2012

Top 88 Times on Mount Marathon
Women Under 60 minutes *(cont'd)*

#	Name	Time	Year		#	Name	Time	Year
29	Nina Kemppel	0:55:08	1996		63	Rachel Dow	0:58:14	2010
30	Nina Kemppel	0:55:08	1997		64	Patti Foldager	0:58:17	1985
31	Allison Barnwell	0:55:08	2012		65	Kathy Anderson	0:58:23	1974
32	Cedar Bourgeois	0:55:09	2004		66	Kjerstln Lastufka	0:58:23	1992
33	Laura Brosius	0:55:18	2010		67	Danielle Pratt	0:58:30	2010
34	Holly Brooks	0:55:29	2008		68	Rachel Dow	0:58:31	2012
35	Carmen Young	0:55:39	1983		69	Nicole DeYong	0:58:40	2008
36	Patti Foldager	0:55:40	1988		70	Sarh Smith	0:58:51	1989
37	Patti Foldager	0:55:48	1987		71	Deborah Nordyke	0:58:52	1987
38	Patti Foldager	0:55:51	1986		72	Aubrey Smith	0:58:57	2008
39	Nancy Pease	0:56:04	1983		73	Cedar Bourgeois	0:59:01	1997
40	Kikkan Randall	0:56:04	2009		74	Nina Kemppel	0:59:06	1993
41	Kjerstln Lastufka	0:56:18	1996		75	Denali Foldager	0:59:07	2012
42	Nancy Pease	0:56:30	1987		76	Kate Fitzgerald	0:59:09	2011
43	Dane HeBallengee	0:56:31	2000		77	Dominique Colberg	0:59:11	2004
44	Patti Foldager	0:56:35	1992		78	Kjerstln Lastufka	0:59:18	1993
45	Patti Foldager	0:56:36	1993		79	Aubrey Smith	0:59:22	2000
46	Nina Kemppel	0:56:46	2003		80	Sheryl Loan	0:59:23	2012
47	Carmen Young	0:56:49	1984		81	Sail Taylor	0:59:32	2010
48	Nina Kemppel	0:56:59	2001		82	Leslie Varys	0:59:34	2011
49	Kikkan Randall	0:57:06	2006		83	Nina Kemppel	0:59:36	1998
50	Carmen Young	0:57:07	1982		84	Aubrey Smith	0:59:37	2009
51	Kjerstln Lastufka	0:57:08	1997		85	Lynn Salanes	0:59:40	1985
52	Kikkan Randall	0:57:08	2005		86	Lauren Fritz	0:59:40	2011
53	Teresa Brady	0:57:25	2000		87	Patti Foldager	0:59:48	1994
54	Betsy Haines	0:57:38	1979		88	Kjerstln Lastufka	0:59:54	1995
55	Kikkan Randall	0:57:38	2001					
56	Allison Spencer	0:57:39	1976					
57	Nina Kemppel	0:57:46	1994					
58	Lisa Corbin	0:57:46	2000					
59	Rachel James	0:57:51	2005					
60	Shannon Donnelly	0:58:05	2004					
61	Liz Carey	0:58:06	1978					
62	Nina Kemppel	0:58:10	1995					

Men Under 46 Minutes

1	Tom Besh	0:45:53	1967	12	Brian Bethard	0:45:47	2004
2	Gene Morgan	0:45:16	1972	13	Trond Flagstad	0:45:52	2005
3	Tom Besh	0:45:49	1973	14	Brian Bethard	0:45:17	2005
4	Jeff Johnson	0:45:32	1976	15	Brad Precosky	0:45:42	2006
5	Bill Spencer	0:45:59	1982	16	Trond Flagstad	0:45:54	2006
6	Bill Spencer	0:45:08	1985	17	Sam Hill	0:45:59	2008
7	Sam Young	0:45:32	1986	18	Eric Strabel	0:45:42	2010
8	Bill Spencer	0:45:32	1986	19	Mark Iverson	0:45:18	2011
9	Todd Boonstra	0:45:17	1997	20	Matias Saari	0:45:13	2012
10	Brad Precosky	0:45:31	2000	21	Ben Ward	0:45:56	2012
11	Brad Precosky	0:45:07	2001				

Men Under 45 Minutes

1	Jonathan Chaffee	0:44:28	1967	8	Trond Flagstad	0:44:03	2008
2	Jonathan Chaffee	0:44:25	1968	9	Trond Flagstad	0:44:40	2010
3	Bill Spencer	0:44:11	1974	10	Eric Strabel	0:44:40	2011
4	Bill Spencer	0:44:37	1975	11	Brent Knight	0:44:58	2011
5	Bill Spencer	0:44:25	1976	12	Matt Novakovich	0:44:07	2012
6	Tom Besh	0:44:59	1977	13	Trond Flagstad	0:44:26	2012
7	Sam Young	0:44:49	1985				

Men Under 44 Minutes

1	Bill Spencer	0:43:21	1981
2	Tobias Schwoerer	0:43:39	2004

www.ingramcontent.com/pod-product-compliance
Lightning Source LLC
LaVergne TN
LVHW051608070426
835507LV00021B/2834